# ONE MAN'S ISRAEL

For my friend Leo
with affection and
my very best wishes.

Neville / 6 July 2008

# ONE MAN'S ISRAEL

## Neville Teller

Trafford
PUBLISHING

Order this book online at www.trafford.com/08-0209
or email orders@trafford.com

Most Trafford titles are also available at major online book retailers.

Note for Librarians: A cataloguing record for this book is available from Library
and Archives Canada at www.collectionscanada.ca/amicus/index-e.html

Printed in Victoria, BC, Canada.

ISBN: 978-1-4251-3754-0

*We at Trafford believe that it is the responsibility of us all, as both individuals
and corporations, to make choices that are environmentally and socially sound.
You, in turn, are supporting this responsible conduct each time you purchase a
Trafford book, or make use of our publishing services. To find out how you are
helping, please visit www.trafford.com/responsiblepublishing.html*

*Our mission is to efficiently provide the world's finest, most comprehensive
book publishing service, enabling every author to experience success.
To find out how to publish your book, your way, and have it available
worldwide, visit us online at www.trafford.com/10510*

 **Trafford** PUBLISHING™ www.trafford.com

**North America & international**
toll-free: 1 888 232 4444 (USA & Canada)
phone: 250 383 6864 ♦ fax: 250 383 6804 ♦ email: info@trafford.com

**The United Kingdom & Europe**
phone: +44 (0)1865 722 113 ♦ local rate: 0845 230 9601
facsimile: +44 (0)1865 722 868 ♦ email: info.uk@trafford.com

10 9 8 7 6 5 4 3 2

*For Sheila,*

*the children and the grandchildren*

# JERUSALEM'S DAY

## by Shmuel Huppert

### English version by Neville Teller from the original Hebrew

Evening rains gentle on a crumbling gate
On stealthy alleys ancient shadows drop
From timeless hate
Darkness weaves a crown of thorns.

The bird of peace spreads blood–tinged wings
On the dark breast of Jerusalem's night
A necklace of light
Shimmering diamonds of desire.

The thumb of night, day's index finger
Lightly hold a blush–red bloom
The rising sun
Yet at your heart the shadows linger.

Mourners at the Wailing Wall
Muezzins calling to believers
Pilgrims trudge the dolorous way
All, all yearning for the day.

# ONE MAN'S ISRAEL

## *Contents*

Jerusalem's Day *(poem)*     vii

Introduction     1

Who Do I Think I Am?     2

Who Is A Jew?     7

The Gathering Storm     12

Five Days Shalt Thou Labour?     15

The Passing Scene – 1
    *(first published in the Jewish Telegraph)*     19

Little Boy Lost *(short story)*     26

The Lavi Down The Drain     34

Holy Rows And Warplanes
    *(first published in The Spectator)*     37

Trying Times     41

Israel's Elgin Marbles     45

The Passing Scene – 2
    *(first published in the Jewish Telegraph)*     48

Vengeance *(short story)*     53

What Is Israel Up To In The Gulf?
    *(first published in the Jewish Herald)*     65

Wishful Thinking?     68

Israel In Black Africa     73

Land Of The Rising Hate
    *(first published in the Jewish Chronicle)*     77

The Passing Scene – 3
    *(first published in the Jewish Telegraph)*      83

What Price Peace?      90

Israel's Day Of Reckoning Is At Hand
    *(first published in the Jewish Telegraph)*      95

Israel's Image - 1
    *(letters to the Jewish Chronicle and the Jerusalem Post)*      99

Israel Speaks To The World      102

Israel's Image - 2
    *(letters to the Jewish Chronicle and the Jerusalem Post)*      108

The Passing Scene - 4
    *(first published in the Jewish Telegraph)*      111

The Case Of Otto Schwarzkopf *(Poem)*      120

The Russians Are Coming      122

The Love Of Books *(short story)*      125

Old City – New Face
    *(first published in the Jewish Chronicle)*      135

The Passing Scene – 5
    *(first published in the Jewish Telegraph)*      140

Monkey Puzzle      144

Return To Masada      146

The Passing Scene – 6
    *(first published in the Jewish Telegraph)*      149

The Orchestra And The People      154

Disgusted Of Tunbridge Wells      159

The Serpent's Smile *(radio play)*      170

**Annex:**

"Jerusalem's Day" – *poem in original Hebrew*      253

"The Suitcase" – *poem in original Hebrew*      *254*

# INTRODUCTION

One man in his time, as we know, plays many parts. With Israel as my theme I have, for the past twenty years, been newspaper columnist, political commentator, correspondent, feature writer, travel writer, short story writer, radio dramatist, and even, on a couple of memorable occasions, translator of Hebrew poetry and, by extension, lyric writer to a Ralph McTell song now immortalised in a CD album.

I have not always written under my own name. Quite early in my parallel career as radio abridger, I found it necessary to choose a *nom-de-plume*, since my BBC producer was getting nervous about the number of commissions I was winning. He thought having my name too often in *Radio Times* looked bad. So I split myself into two – Neville Teller and Edmund Owen (the name an amalgam of my Oxford college, St Edmund Hall, and my school, Owen's). Much later, when I was a civil servant and began writing about that political hot potato, Israel, it seemed judicious (to use a civil service term) to revert to my *alter ego* for these journalistic activities.

So, not only did articles appear in the *Spectator* and the *Jewish Herald* under the name Edmund Owen, but for quite some time "Edmund Owen's Israel" – a column devoted to observations of the passing scene – was a feature of the *Jewish Telegraph* (published weekly in Manchester). As for the pieces I wrote for the *Jewish Chronicle*, they were never political in tone, and those I signed with my real name.

Inevitably, for every piece published there were many which, for one reason or another, never graced the printed page – or, indeed, the airwaves. Taken together, though, the selection of the published and unpublished that I bring together in this book chart my changing personal perceptions of the kaleidoscopic Israeli scene over the past twenty years. I've arranged for the political and descriptive pieces to follow a loose chronology, so as to allow an impression of the changing Israeli scene to emerge. And I start with pieces which paint a picture of Israel as it appeared to me twenty years ago.

My take on Israeli life and politics will probably seem idiosyncratic at times, but I hope that if this man's view of Israel does not quite accord with yours, it may at least provide some entertainment, even if – or, more likely, when – you violently disagree.

As a sort of *hors d'oeuvre* to the main meal, I thought I would try to explain where I am coming from, as a Jew and an Israel-watcher. The opportunity to do so rests in three pieces of writing. One, which I felt moved to write in 1991 and did not submit for publication, I called "Who Do I Think I Am?" The other two are letters published respectively in the *Jewish Chronicle* in December 2004, and in the *Guardian* in August 2002.

\*

# WHO DO I THINK I AM?

Who admits to being typical – "of a type"? Not me, for one. Most people, and I'm among them, believe they are uniquely themselves, and that their opinions, equally, are theirs alone.

Who am I? My grandparents came to England from the Pale of Settlement, that middle European hinterland created after the Tsar had swallowed up a chunk of Poland, and with it over a million Jews. My father arrived here as a boy; my mother was born in this country. These personal details are shared, more or less, by a thousand other English Jews.

Does that make me typical?

Let me fill in the background.

Born, bred and educated in London, my mother loved this country. She sympathised with its inherent traditions of decency and tolerance; she loved its countryside; above all she cherished its literature. For a time she trained to be a teacher but, her course cut short by ill health during the First World War, she served for a while as a land girl and then in the Civil Service. But she remained an avid reader, and she imparted to her only son something of her own delight in English literature – a delight that in her youth had represented a window of escape from the grimmer realities of the immigrants' East End.

My father was observant, if not exactly orthodox. Our household was strictly kosher, he never worked on the sabbath, we observed the festivals and Holy Days. On the other hand, he was not to be seen in synagogue all that often on a Saturday and in my youth the occasional outing on a Saturday afternoon was not unknown.

Typical? Only in externals. Otherwise, me – an English Jew, a product of my personal background and upbringing. So I claim to speak for no-one but myself.

It is natural enough to love the land of one's birth and upbringing, and like my mother, I do. I have come also to love Israel. With a married son and his family living in Jerusalem, we come and go several times each year. My granddaughters are *sabras*. It is a genuine second home. So the gulf that seems to yawn perpetually between Britain and Israel on the issues that matter most to me as a Jew is a constant anguish. Those feelings, at least, I know I share with many other English Jews.

Yet I have come to realise that my twin loyalties are far from irreconcilable. The key to understanding is in averting one's gaze, temporarily at least, from the twists and turns of the political spinning–top and considering, as coolly and clear-headedly as possible, what it is that divides and what unites the "English" and the "Jew" in us.

Examine the differences between Britain and Israel. They are now, as they have always been, essentially political – and therefore, by definition, ephemeral if not precisely superficial. They are bound up with current political imperatives which can, as recent events in Europe and the Soviet Union demonstrate, be overturned in an amazingly short time.

From the days of Empire, Britain has had an historic need to maintain viable relations with at least part of the Arab and Muslim worlds in the Middle East. She has done so with varying degrees of enthusiasm for a century and a half. But only examine the history of that relationship, and it is revealed as a shifting miasma of alliances and understandings, blown here and there by the changing demands of political expediency. How could it be otherwise, when relations between the Arab states themselves are a kaleidoscope of constantly changing patterns? *Realpolitik* governs this, as it governs all other aspects of Britain's foreign policy – and, indeed, the foreign policies of all States. If political history has any lesson to teach us, it is that self–interest is always the guiding principle in relations between States.

Now look at what binds together the English tradition and the Jew.

These bonds are so strong and lie so deep that they are virtually indestructible. This country's way of life, secular as well as religious, rests on the self–same moral base as the Jewish religion. However odd the concept may seem, the fact of the matter is that the commandments and statutes and judgements which Moses handed down to the Children of Israel are as integral to the structure of Britain's institutions as they are to Israel's; they are as embedded in the very fabric of our society here as they are in the Jewish religion.

Britain may be less of a Christian nation in a number of ways than it was a century ago. To that extent, perhaps, the Old Testament may have lost some formal authority within the fabric of the country. But despite that, the underlying moral values of the Bible are so inherent in every aspect of our own values, our political and judicial institutions, our literature and our way of life, that they cannot be gainsaid: the sanctity of life, the priority of right over might, the over-riding concepts of justice and compassion for the vulnerable and disenfranchised.

No amount of transient political manoeuvering or misunderstanding, no dissension however deep between this country and Israel, can change that immutable fact. Strong as the political bonds may at times appear to be between Britain and some declared enemy of Israel, that common moral stock from which both traditions spring represents a rock–solid bridge between my Englishness and my Jewishness that only some unforeseeable cataclysm could ever shake.

*

The Editor,
The Jewish Chronicle

Sir,

My experience of anti–Semitism and British life largely mirrors Robert Winston's (JC, December 24). 1 encountered very little anti–Semitism at school, in the army, at Oxford University, or in a career spent variously in marketing, publishing, the Civil Service, a national charity and the BBC.

Lately, I have taken to wondering whether it was my mother's influence that provided me with some sort of protection.

My mother was educated – and later became a pupil–teacher – at the Jews' Free School in the early 1900s, when Louis Abrahams was headmaster. The JFS, while rooted firmly in the Orthodox tradition, inculcated in its 2,500 pupils a reverence for things British – from a wide knowledge and love of English literature and history, to pride in the legal, cultural and military achievements of the nation that had won, and then ruled, an empire on which the sun never set.

The school, founded as early as 1822, later came to see as its *raison d'être* the Anglicisation of the largely immigrant, Yiddish–speaking youngsters who poured through its doors. Louis Abrahams spoke of "wiping away all evidence of foreign birth."

I am coming to perceive the extent to which those influences, imbibed by my mother, worked on me during my own childhood. In passing on to me the intense pleasure she gained from English literature, she also imparted not a little of that feeling, so strong in her own upbringing, of belonging here in Britain, and being proud to do so, without in any way compromising one's Judaism.

It takes two to tango. At various periods during my life "institutional" anti–Semitism in Britain has been more overt than at others, and anti-Semitic activity – malevolent or mindless – on the increase or the decline. But I have been either too conditioned, or too thick–skinned, to note or respond to anti–Semitism that may, or may not, have been directed personally against me.

*31 December 2004*

\*

The Editor,
The Guardian

Sir,

Like your correspondents (Letter, August 8), 1 am a Jew born and raised outside Israel. I cherish the fact that, after more than 2,000 years, I have the right to belong to a Jewish state, lawfully constituted by a vote of the UN. I value this right, the dream of generations of my people, because:

1) Israel is a genuine multicultural democracy, with people from every ethnic background, including over a million Arab citizens who chose to remain when the state was declared, and with Arab members of parliament.

2) Jews should be free to live anywhere in the world including Israel and, indeed, any Muslim state. The time for *"Judenfrei"*

areas should have died with Hitler. Arabs live freely in Israel. In how many Arab countries are Jews permitted to live their lives similarly? Jews are still victims of racial apartheid in a large part of the Arab world.

3) Israel occupies the West Bank and Gaza because the territories were overrun during a war initiated by a combination of Arab forces intent on destroying Israel. Since that time, Egypt has renounced sovereignty over Gaza, and Jordan over the West Bank. The areas, in international law, currently belong to no one. Only a political agreement, involving the establishment of a Palestinian sovereign state, can resolve the situation. This time – unlike in 1947 – let us hope Arab leaders will allow this UN resolve to take effect.

*9 August 2002*

*

The months leading to Israel's 40th anniversary in 1988 saw the re-emergence of an issue that had dogged the State since its foundation (and which, as my letter to the Guardian revealed, dogs it still) – who is a Jew?

# WHO IS A JEW?

On the face of it Susan Miller, a dumpy middle–aged American woman, unglamorous and without much money, has little in common with Elizabeth Taylor. What they share is that, like thousands of others each year, they were converted to Judaism. Elizabeth Taylor, who became Jewish to marry the late Mike Todd, may have lapsed from the faith; Susan Miller (or Shoshana, as she prefers to be called) is at the centre of a religio–political controversy that has dogged the

State of Israel very nearly from its birth, and has continued to rock it at intervals ever since.

Shoshana Miller's story is quickly told. She was converted in America by a Reform rabbi in order to marry a Jew. Later she decided to emigrate to Israel. The Minister of the Interior – an ultra-orthodox rabbi himself and a member of the extreme religious party, Shas – refused to register her as a Jewess, on the grounds that only conversions undertaken in strict accordance with orthodox practice (the "halacha") are valid. Shoshana Miller appealed to the High Court, which ruled against the Minister, Yitzhak Peretz, who promptly resigned.

The implications of the High Court ruling were that all new immigrants who have converted to Judaism, no matter through what procedure, must be registered as Jews – which is precisely the situation obtaining before Rabbi Peretz assumed charge of the Interior Ministry.

The issue itself, though, and what lies behind it, has rumbled on for forty years. The umpteenth attempt by Israel's religious parties to introduce a "Who is a Jew" Bill was defeated only a few days before the Knesset rose for the summer recess. Undeterred, the three members of Shas immediately tabled an amendment to a current Act which would effectively have achieved the same results, threatening, if they didn't get their way, to upset the delicate political balance that keeps the Likud Government in power until the prescribed time of the next General Election.

When that too failed, another tack was immediately tried. The idea this time was to manipulate the regulatory powers that attach to the Interior Ministry and force immigrant converts to file their conversion documents with the Population Registry. That too fizzled out when it became clear that the Law Committee would never approve. So the issue goes into storage – one can scarcely say "on ice" in a summer that is turning into one of the hottest on record – and in the autumn the long–drawn–out struggle will doubtless be rejoined.

What is it all about? Hitler had few doubts about who a Jew was. One grandparent with "Jewish blood", and the Nuremberg Laws applied. Although an apparently catch–all definition, in fact the Nazi view of Judaism was essentially a rather narrow one.

Neither Elizabeth Taylor nor Shoshana Miller would have qualified – though they would certainly have fallen foul of the Race Laws on other grounds. But what would the high priests of Nazi theology have made of a Jewish state that continually comes to the brink of denying the designation "Jew" to Americans whose parents and grandparents were indubitably of Jewish blood back to the thousandth generation? Or that is content at the same time to clutch to the bosom of Judaism the Falashas from the heart of Africa, entirely negroid in appearance, whose religious practices, if not their Jewish antecedents, are to some extent dubious?

These apparent anomalies are features of modern Israel precisely because the criteria now being used to define "Jew" have little of race in them. Israel – both as a nation state and as the corpus of Jewish thought – denies that there is such a thing as a "Jewish race". A stroll along Tel Aviv's Dizengoff any day should be enough to explain why. The in–gathering of the past 40 years has revealed the enormous diversity of racial types that go to make up the Jewish people.

The various dispersions from the Holy Land, which started some 3,000 years ago, scattered Jews across the face of the earth in wave after wave. Wherever they settled in sufficient numbers to enable their religion and the way of life based upon it to be practised, the slow process of genetic assimilation inevitably began, however power-ful the social pressures against it. As a result Israel today is an extraor-dinary amalgam – the world in a pepperpot. People of every shade of skin and exhibiting virtually every racial characteristic make up modern Israeli society, living refutations of the crude pre-war Nazi caricatures of "the Jew".

The religio–political query "Who is a Jew?" stems from the Law of Return – a founding principle of the state which was formally enacted in 1950. It guarantees citizenship automatically to any Jew who wants it. A *raison d'être* of the State of Israel was to restore a homeland to the Jewish people; after their age–long sojourn in the wilderness they were to come again to the promised land. In the more practical terms of 1948, it sought to put an end to the intolerable sufferings of the ex–inmates of the concentration camps. Now designated "displaced persons", they were still, three years after the Allied victory, crowded into refugee camps in conditions only marginally better than the camps from which they had been liberated,

In the early days few questions were asked. No–one was particularly eager to claim Jewish blood if they were not in fact of Jewish origin, and under the pressure of the times there was little inclination to probe into the detail of individual claims. In Jewish religious law the transmission of Judaism passes through the mother. If one's mother is Jewish, one is a Jew regardless of the origin of one's father (a sensible protective measure which held embattled Jewish communities together after the recurrent episodes of progrom, pillage and rape to which they have been subjected over the centuries).

But Judaism is a religious spectrum ranging from an orthodoxy of mind–boggling inflexibility to a liberality so lax that it seems scarcely to touch Jewish custom beyond a partiality to the occasional bowl of chicken soup. Needless to say, the corpus of Jewish religious tradition is jealously guarded in its pristine form by the orthodox wing of the faith which, because of this, claims to be the arbiter of the criteria that determine the status "Jew".

In religious terms, they already enjoy that power in respect of anyone wishing to be recognised within the orthodox arm of the faith. Persons married or converted to Judaism by virtue of procedures, or by rabbis, not adhering to the "halacha" are not validly married or converted in their eyes.

America contains the largest Jewish community in the world – greater by two million than the State of Israel itself. Only a small proportion – no more than 10 per cent – are orthodox; most are from Conservative, Reform or even more way–out branches. These each have their own rabbis and apply their own procedures in such matters as marriage and conversion to Judaism. No such marriages or conversions are, of course, recognised by the orthodox wing of the faith, either outside Israel or within.

.Herein lies the crux of the problem. Conversions to orthodox Judaism are few and far between; conversions to the less strict wings of the faith, usually to facilitate a marriage, are much more easily arranged. But are such converts, and even more to the point, are their children, "Jews" in the sense that they fall within the scope of the Law of Return? "No" say the bastions of orthodoxy within Israel; "yes" say the civil authorities.

The individual *causes célèbres*, the battles waged and the political in–fighting over the issue have been long and are far from over. Cases which came to the Supreme Court in the 1950s and 1960s resulted in a law which defined "Jew" as "person born to a Jewish mother, or who has been converted to Judaism and is not a member of another religion." Of course that begs the question, and it is to have the words "in accordance with the halacha" included after "Judaism" that the religious interests have mounted an unremitting campaign ever since.

The implications if they succeed would be that large numbers of people all over the world who are, on every conceivable criterion except the strictly orthodox one, Jewish through and through, would be denied the status of Jew in Israeli law and be relegated to second–class or even non-Jewish status. And this would include the majority of the vastly influential and wealthy American Jewish community. The potential effects on domestic American politics, on Israel and on the Middle East as a whole if Israel's religious minority were to get its way, are incalculable.

*

In early 1987 Shamir's Likud government was clinging, rather desperately, to the lifeboat of the "Greater Israel" concept that was breaking up beneath its feet. These were the dying months of what we now see as the pre-"Two-State Solution" era. Talk of an international peace conference was in the air – a conference at which, by common consent, the Palestinians would not be directly represented. I wrote "The Gathering Storm" in May 1987.

# THE GATHERING STORM

You always know the time in Israel. From the Golan to Eilat the country vibrates on the hour to the radio time signal. Walk down a suburban street in Haifa, Tel Aviv or Jerusalem and you are pursued by the pips from apartment to apartment. The fact is, Israel is obsessive about current events. News dominates daily life. Even the buses are fitted with radios. For most of the time they are kept fairly low to entertain the driver, but on the hour, as the first pip sounds, it is the invariable practice to turn the volume up so that everyone on board can be quite sure of catching the news. The bus companies know what the travelling public wants.

For the past few weeks Israelis have been agog to hear the latest exchanges in the Demjanjuk trial, which has turned into a sort of gigantic soap opera being played out for real before the nation. However nature abhors a vacuum, and with the trial in recess a new topic of obsessive interest has flooded in to fill the gap – the "international peace conference".

What conference? There is perhaps nothing surprising in political wiseacres, in Israel as elsewhere, devoting hours of airtime and acres of newsprint to exhaustive analysis of the nonexistent, and episodes of less significance have shaken Governments – as, indeed, the Israeli Government has been shaken in the past fortnight. Talk of a possible general election has been rife. And over what? Over a fragile chimera – the concept of a gathering to be attended by permanent members of the Security Council, Israel and leading Arab powers to discuss moves towards a permanent peace in the Middle East.

How much is substance and how much shadow? Shimon Peres, rotated last autumn out of the premiership into the role of opposition Foreign Secretary under the 1984 General Election deal struck with the Likud, has certainly been indulging in high powered activity both in Washington and with King Hussein in several undisclosed locations. There is evidence that he reached some sort of understanding with the king about who might sit round the table – if a gathering to discuss the peace process were ever convened – and perhaps something of what they might talk about, although as soon as a hint of a deal emerged recently the Jordanians were swift to repudiate the notion.

Word emanating from Kuwait suggests that Gorbachev has given a kind of guarantee to President Assad that Soviet participation would be made conditional on Syria's presence at the table.

The story from Washington at the start of the saga was that the administration was anxious to push the Peres initiative forward, but afraid to intervene too openly in a situation which might swiftly develop into a major political crisis in Israel. As the likelihood of a Government dissolution receded, Washington grew bolder. Now it seems that delegates from the US and the USSR will actually be starting discussions during June around the possibilities. The US team will reportedly be led by Assistant Secretary of State Richard Murphy.

Out of these ingredients a heady political brew has fermented. Prime Minister Yitzhak Shamir and the Likud, not only from political persuasion but because they depend on the support of the minority religious parties, remain resolutely opposed to handing back territory on the West Bank or in Gaza – a basic element in Labour Alignment thinking. They take their stand on the Camp David accords reached between Egypt and Israel during the Begin era, and refuse to step beyond the line of eventual autonomy for the Arab inhabitants of occupied territories. While unable to prevent Shimon Peres from probing the possibilities of an international gathering to discuss a peace settlement, the Premier made it plain that there would be no Government backing for any initiative which had as its central plank land in exchange for peace.

Could Peres deliver the international conference all the hooha is about? He probably doubts that himself now. The Jordanians appear equivocal, and Hussein naturally remains ever wary of moving too close to a rapprochement with Israel, having in mind, as he must, the fate of others who tried and were gunned down for their efforts. The king's fractured relations with Yasser Arafat, too, are far from repaired, and in an international forum in which Arafat would not be personally present, the king might actually appear to him as a competitor for the leadership of the Palestinian interest. As a PLO presence at the table would not be acceptable, even to Shimon Peres, the question of a Palestinian representation acceptable to Yasser Arafat, to say nothing of those of the PLO leadership less accommodating than he, would also need to be resolved.

Gorbachov's guarantee to Syria raises also the question of Soviet–Israeli relations. Israel's national unity coalition are united at least on the need for some clear signs of a thaw on Jewish issues before Russian participation in a conference would be acceptable. The thaw is sought on two fronts: the restoration of diplomatic relations and the easing of restrictions on Soviet Jews, especially on the emigration issue. Although there have been hopeful indications on both, for the present indications are all they are.

Clearly, then, any international peace gathering involving the USSR is some way off. This did not prevent an internal Israeli political crisis of near–cataclysmic proportions developing over the past two weeks. Israel's national unity coalition is a Government held in quivering balance by means of a complex of internal tensions. The peace plan proposals, which Peres insisted on bringing to the inner cabinet but which he did not press to the point of resignation, have demonstrated the irreconcilable difference of approach between the two main partners on the central issue of peace in the region.

Under Israel's constitution early elections are possible only by way of a majority vote in the Knesset, and the Labour grouping cannot count on a majority for this purpose. If Peres pulled down the Government without winning a vote for new elections, there is no guarantee at all that Yitzhak Shamir would not be back a few weeks later at the head of a new and realigned Government.

So for the moment the febrile coalition stays put, Shamir and the Likud rule, the international peace gathering, like the ghost of Hamlet's father, appears and disappears from the scene but undoubtedly remains a key element in the unfolding drama. Meanwhile Shimon Peres, the gloomy Israeli, ponders future action.

*

During that long, hot summer of 1987, the turmoil in the body politic spilled over into the strictly domestic scene. Strikes in the public sector brought acute discomfort to the whole population. Then the Government came up with a cunning wheeze.

## *FIVE* DAYS SHALT THOU LABOUR?

Israel is suffering an attack of what used to be called "the British disease" – an epidemic not of bronchitis but of strikes. Strikes in the public sector, to be precise. With recent Tory election broadcasts highlighting our own winter of discontent still vivid, we might spare a thought for Israel's public. In Israel it is the summer that seems to bring out the worst in industrial relations.

Personal dealings with the public sector in Israel in any of its manifestations is a trial at the best of times. Over recent weeks a series of whole–day strikes has elevated public sector *laissez–faire* into an art form. Hardened, by and large, to offices one expects open and functioning being inexplicably closed and deserted, the Israeli public could be expected to shrug its long–suffering shoulders. But deprive your Israeli on the Petah Tikva omnibus of his TV, or worse his radio with its consistent on–the–hour news bulletins, and you are indeed hitting him where it hurts. So far in the present dispute Kol Israel has been off the air for three separate days.

This year the wage round has been somewhat more fraught than usual. The tug of war has been between the Histadrut – the Israeli version of what a much-inflated TUC might have become had history taken a different turn – and the Government. The issue: salary rises to take account of what is now an annual inflation rate of only 12%–18%.

Into last year's negotiating round the concept of a national minimum wage was suddenly introduced, before it all ended in a settlement on less radical lines. This year the Government has suddenly offered the concession of a 2–day weekend in exchange for a reasonable settlement on wage levels.

Surprising as it may seem in what, to all outward appearances, is a fully–functioning advanced Western society, Israel still operates a 5½–day working week that the rest of the developed world has long since abandoned. In fact, for many it is a 5¾-day week.

Early each Friday afternoon the country more or less shuts up shop so as to prepare for the Sabbath, which comes in at dusk. As visitors to Israel will know, outside the main tourist centres and the Arab areas, Saturday in Israel resembles nothing so much as Sunday in Welsh chapel–land or in wee Frees country beyond the border.

But then in Israel the Sabbath lasts only until the first stars appear in the sky, so come nightfall the buses start again, the cinemas, shops, restaurants and street cafes open, and people flock out to just as riotous a Saturday night as you are likely to enjoy in London, Paris or New York. The only problem is that Sunday is a normal working day, and Israelis have long become inured to the idea that the Monday morning syndrome is far worse when it happens on a Sunday.

The 5–day working week on offer, therefore, is a Sunday–to–Thursday version. Since banks and offices close shortly after midday on Friday anyway, runs the Government's argument, why not go the whole hog (even though hogs indubitably fall into the category of the non–kosher)? For openers the Histadrut professes to be unimpressed, and is attempting to confine the discussion to cash on the table.

Israel is not Jerusalem, but in Jerusalem and its suburbs the Sabbath is a peculiarly complex affair. Three religions, three different days of the week observed as the Sabbath – a recipe for confusion. The general introduction of a 5–day working week that results in a shut–down on Friday as well as Saturday would do nothing for the Christian communities, but might go some way towards improving Arab-Jewish relations in the city.

At the moment observant Muslims are affronted by "business as usual" on Friday mornings, or by Jews or Christians invading their neighbourhoods on their Sabbath. The same is true for observant Jews on Saturdays who, in the closely–packed Old City for example, have to endure the same crowds of tourists flocking into the Arab market – the Shouk – as during the rest of the week. A 5–day working week might remove – or at least alleviate – some of the current irritations – though doubtless at the expense of all the others. How long, one wonders, before the more enterprising banks and stores would begin finding ways around the commercial disadvantages of a 2–day shut–down, just like in Britain? Could all the Post Offices really take a 2–day break every week?

The lesson from the West is that a 5–day working week is fine, just provided it is not the same 5 days for everybody. That is not a concept likely to go down well in a society like Israel, where the religious influence is strong and the Sabbath is the Sabbath and no messing.

The reason why the proposal is quite likely to go through is because, like all the best political formulae, it provides a face–saving solution to a nagging difficulty, and it also meets the hidden aspirations of those apparently in dispute. The circumstances uncannily parallel the byzantine negotiations that accompany public sector wage negotiations in this country, where civil servants representing management sit across the table from other civil servants representing labour and engage in earnest acrimony. So in Israel it is perfectly understood that the proposal to close down public sector offices all·day Friday is code for permitting everyone in the public sector extra time to devote to the moonlighting.

For few are the public servants – or indeed, anyone else in Israel – who has only one source of income. Standards of living would be impossible. A typical senior radio executive working for Kol Yisrael has a salary not much greater than £7,000. No wonder he or she also directs on contract for the Habimah Theatre, or writes scripts for European TV companies, or owns a vineyard.

Moonlighting runs very deep in Israeli society. Students on grants do it – no questions asked – to work their way, American fashion, through college via a string of jobs as waiters or washers–up. The taxi driver taking you to Ben Gurion airport could have sold you your ticket to New York three hours earlier. Bank clerks doing evening duty in the luxury hotels can turn the following morning into university lecturers, and vice versa.

It is well understood that the level of public sector salaries is ludicrously low – perhaps as a consequence of the gross over-manning. For the present it would not be economically feasible to raise them to anything like a reasonable level. Quite the reverse. It is of course part of the Government's strategy to hold increases at, or if possible below, the level of inflation. The only ploy left is, as it were, to formalise the enormous wink the Government already gives to the copious variety of ways the salaried sector has adopted to achieve an acceptable standard of living. Hence the machiavellian cunning that lies beneath the latest offer – an offer the unions are going to find great difficulty in refusing.

*

For several years in the late-1980s, as a regular columnist for the *Jewish Telegraph*, I commented on the highways and by-ways of Israeli life. These observations, which appeared under the generic title: "Edmund Owen's Israel", aimed to give something · of the flavour of Israeli life to the reader in far-off Britain.

# THE PASSING SCENE – 1

Strolling down Jaffa in Jerusalem I turned, as one does, into Steimatzky's for a browse. You don't normally expect to see the telephone directory on sale in your high street, but unmistakeably a pile of Jerusalem directories, priced at about £4, were nestling alongside the marked–down fiction.

Closer examination revealed that this publication was not the standard version, but an English translation. What a splendid idea! I waylaid the chief buyer and asked her all about it.

"The runaway publishing success of the year," she declared. "Where Jerusalem leads, the rest of Israel will surely follow."

The venture is not without its problems. All Jerusalem's telephone subscribers were circulated with a card on which they were asked to transliterate their names into English. The result is not, to English eyes, particularly logical. For example, the same Hebrew name can appear as Meir, Mayer or Meyer. Still, half a loaf is certainly better than no bread, and even though there are no yellow pages, as in the Hebrew version of the directory, it is a great blessing to the *oleh chadash* (new immigrant), or visitor, to be able to look up a number without seeking help.

Unfortunately, since publication there has been yet another change–round of telephone numbers in the Jerusalem area, and for some subscribers the prefix 5 has been altered to 3. So if you dial the number you find in the English edition, there's a chance you'll get nothing better than the unobtainable signal.

*

Staying in Ramot Eshkol for a bit, I can't help observing that a feature of life in the northern suburbs of Jerusalem is the regular call of the muezzins from the hilltop mosque towers that dominate the Arab villages on the Nablus road. Nowadays they are transmission by loudspeaker of what are usually taped recordings. Each broadcast lasts five or ten minutes and consists of singing and chanting, sometimes with several voices. Often one mosque follows another in sequence.

The first transmission is at four o'clock in the morning, and whether one becomes aware of it or not depends in large measure on the direction of the wind.

I suppose the nearest parallel in the UK would be the sound of church bells. The comparison breaks down since, in this case, every day is Sunday – and Friday, the Muslim day of rest, even more so. Like every other aspect of life in modern Israel, it is something one can grow to live with and even, after a fashion, appreciate. Especially as it's a living, daily reminder of the religious tolerance that is a cornerstone of the State.

*

In what other country would the armed services publish a quarterly magazine for the public in which the defense of the nation is discussed in detail and at length, and the latest weaponry fully described and illustrated?

About to celebrate its fifth birthday is the IDF Journal, produced since 1982 by the Israel Defense Forces. There is nothing quite like it in the UK. The glossy magazine carries a surprising amount of advertising, ranging from Bank Leumi to – fascinating in itself – computerised weapons systems.

But the shock to British eyes is the editorial content where, in detailed articles, military experts and top-ranking officers of the IDF discuss – with what seems like an amazing lack of discretion – matters like Israel's participation in Star Wars, current ideas about integrating airpower into ground–based military operations to ensure success in any future Air-Land Battle, and current thinking on what is known as C3I (Command and Control, Communications and Intelligence).

The whole venture is either the biggest security breach of all time or – much more likely – the cleverest device yet contrived to demonstrate at home and abroad the extent and depth of Israel's military capability.

*

Talking of battles, I attended a teach–in by leading health promotion experts in Tel Aviv, to learn that one war Israel is fighting in alliance with the rest of the world is the one against tobacco.

The decrease in smoking among Israelis over the past five years is quite marked – even the buses are smoke–free these days. Nevertheless the adult smoking rate is considerably higher than in the USA or the UK, and though the population seems partly protected from heart attacks (because, experts believe, of its Mediterranean diet rich in fish and olive oil), the rate of lung cancer is causing concern.

Health warnings on cigarette packs and promotional material are obligatory, but public health experts are concerned because in newspaper advertisements the warnings still appear only in tiny type and represent less than 1 per cent of the available space, unlike the 17.5 per cent in the UK.

But Israel is ahead of the game in a new struggle – this time against tobacco packaged in tiny pouches and intended to be held in the mouth and sucked. The habit, known as "snuff dipping", has spread widely in the USA and some Scandinavian countries, has been introduced into this country, and is known to be associated with mouth cancer.

A leading role in convincing the Israeli Government to prohibit its import was played by Dr Cheri Papier of the Sackler Faculty of Medicine of Tel Aviv University. She was convinced the only way to avoid a future epidemic of oral cancer in Israel was to ensure this type of product never gained a foothold in the first place.

I met Dr Papier in the University and she took me through the case she had prepared, which finally convinced the Government to ban the product.

"I felt a tremendous sense of urgency," she told me. "We had to act before it was too late."

\*

You can't help noticing the re–designed public telephone booth that is starting to make its appearance on Israeli streets. To anyone who has ever struggled to get through using some of Israel's ancient public telephones, where the dials are stuck on every which-way, the dial–stops cut your finger like tin-openers, and the machine's appetite for asimonim can only be compared with a walrus's for fish, this is welcome indeed.

Simple and elegant is the best way to describe the new telephone booth. Gone are the dials. A push–button connection system is attached to the front of a slim blue column that rests on a square base. A protective transparent shield and sides are wrapped around the operative parts.

There is also hope of actually getting through more often and more correctly when you do push the buttons. The telephone company, Bezek, is a year into a five–year plan to replace its outmoded exchanges with brand new digital switching equipment. The first digital switching exchanges have already been installed. British Telecom watch out!

*

Shabbat service schedules of the average Israeli synagogue represent an endless topic of conversation among British and American visitors. To diaspora Jews brought up on a tradition of walking home from synagogue to a lateish 1.30pm lunch, the idea of getting through the Shabbat service, discourse and all, and being back home for an early 8 am breakfast is a fascinating topsy–turvy situation that adds a special piquancy to a visit to Israel.

It is when the realisation dawns that Israeli synagogues normally undertake *two* such services in sequence each Shabbat morning, and that the building is nevertheless empty and silent by 9.30am, that your visitor begins asking how they do it.

Minyan Aleph will make a 6.30 or 6.45 o'clock start, while minyan Bet will be ready for the off by 7.45 or 8. Two Shacharits, two laiyenings, two haftoras, two discourses, two Mussafs – and all done by a quarter past nine!

How can it possibly take us up to three hours in England to undertake what it is commonplace to achieve in Israel in half the time? And with no discernible lack of fervour or decorum.

Visitors from the West endlessly ask whether we are not all, perhaps, wedded to some 18th century Russian or Polish time schedule – or even some 19th century concept based on Sunday morning church services. Perhaps there's a case for returning to our roots, rising reasonably early on Shabbat and getting on with the business in hand. It's a thought!

*

Where else but in Israel would you find an open–air café with gaily striped umbrellas, an impressive brand new promenade, lawns, a car park and tourist buses rolling up every few minutes – all in the middle of nowhere?

Some enterprising entrepreneur has constructed all this out of what was, only a year ago, a refuse heap. The point is that the refuse heap in question – just off the main Derech Hebron on the road leading to East Talpiot and close by a UN Observation Post – commanded perhaps the most impressive view of Jerusalem available anywhere. Hence what is the most extraordinary development I think I have seen – the Haas Promenade.

On the evening I visited it, the car park was jammed solid, there were seven tourist coaches in evidence, the viewing platform and the whole promenade were packed with sightseers. And then, incredibly, across the green came a bride in full wedding gown with bridesmaids, accompanied by the *chatan* (groom) and best man.

"What on earth is going on?" I asked a bystander.

"Don't you know the old Jerusalem custom?" he replied. "A few days before the wedding the bride and groom visit their favourite places in full wedding costume. This has always been a hot favourite (I did some of my own courting here), but it was a bit much for the pre–wedding visit when there was a rubbish tip just over there. Now..."

And I saw what he meant. Not only is the view absolutely breathtaking, but what is now the Haas Promenade – in the middle of nowhere though it is – is indeed fit for a bride. It's like a chunk of the front at Southport, without the sea.

\*

Talking of sea–fronts, the city authorities of Tel Aviv have recently permitted a visual display calculated to knock you sideways.

The sea frontage of the Dan Hotel consists of a long series of upright concrete pillars interspersed with vertical panels. I was astounded, as I approached it along the promenade from a distance, to see that the hotel took on the appearance of a complete rainbow spectrum, from violet to orange through shades of blue, green, yellow and scarlet. As you get closer the different colours open out until, facing the hotel square on, you see that the whole frontage has been painted in such a way that the colours have been made to merge gradually into one another.

Heaven knows how the hotel got development permission for this extravaganza. It certainly makes a feature well worth looking out for.

*

It was while I was walking along the wide seafront promenade at Tel Aviv one day, watching the animated scene and the crowded beaches, that I suddenly remembered an incident that happened to me on Bournemouth beach when I was very small. For a few brief, but terrifying, minutes, as I turned from paddling at the water's edge, I couldn't see the familiar faces of my family seated in their deckchairs on the sand. I'd wandered a few feet along the beach, and I was now facing a vast alien crowd. I was lost and alone! The episode was soon over, and in minutes I was back among the people I knew and loved – but it's one of those experiences that remain with you all your life. As the memory returned, that afternoon in Tel Aviv, the idea for a story suddenly came into my mind...

# LITTLE BOY LOST

You know what they say about the sea–front at Tel Aviv. Walk along it often enough, and you're bound to meet everyone you've ever known.

On a July afternoon in the mid–1960s the beaches running south from Kikkar Atarim were packed. Children were scampering up and down to the sea over the blistering sand and mothers were screaming at them. The ice–cream sellers and the life–guards were doing a roaring trade. The scene was vivid in the brilliant sunshine – coloured umbrellas, red–and–yellow sun shelters, striped deck chairs. In the midst of it all a woman, not young not old, in a long–sleeved blue dress with polka dots and a little white collar and cuffs, was gazing to left and right. She bit her knuckles in a vain attempt to stifle a sob.

"My God, what am I going to do? What can I do?"

She spoke to herself, for there was no one with her, but it chanced that the words were overheard by a fair–haired young man in his twenties carrying a towel, who had just stepped on to the sands.

"In some sort of trouble?" he said. "What's the problem?"

Although she partly turned her head in his direction, she scarcely seemed to hear him for the long half–controlled sobs that were now welling up from deep within her.

"What shall 1 do? Who can I turn to?"

"Perhaps I can help?" said the young man, for he had a kind heart.

"I don't know."

She looked distractedly from side to side.

"Why don't you tell me about it?" The young man took a handkerchief from his pocket. "Here."

She accepted it and dabbed at her eyes.

"Thank you. You're so kind."

She made to give it back.

"No, no," said the young man. "Keep it. Now, what's happened?"

As if emboldened by his concern, the woman clutched at his arm.

"It's terrible, terrible. My little boy – Danny – he seems to have wandered off."

"Wandered off? You mean, he's lost?"

The woman nodded, and could not stop another sob. She pressed both hands to her cheeks.

"Yes, he's lost. What am I to do? Tell me what I can do."

The young man kept his cool.

"He can't have gone far. When did you last see him?"

The woman was vague.

"I don't quite know. I was just sitting here. Then I looked up, and he wasn't there."

Seized by a sudden spasm of energy, she called down the beach towards the sea, her voice mingling with the cries of the children and the portable radios:

"Danny! Danny! Where are you?"

"Come on," said the young man, abandoning thoughts of stripping to the bathing trunks he wore beneath his slacks and snoozing in the sun. "I'll help you look for him. What does he look like, Mrs...?"

He looked at her enquiringly.

"Weiss," she said. "My name is Weiss. Oh, he's a most beautiful child. Soft, fair hair. Blue eyes – blue like the sea. Blue, just like yours."

"And how old?"

"Four," said Mrs Weiss. "He's four years old."

"That's very young. We must find him quickly."

She seemed disturbed by his reaction, and her hand flew to her mouth as a new thought suddenly struck her.

"The sea! Could he have wandered into the sea? Oh, my God!"

The young man kept his head.

"Was he wearing a bathing costume?"

"No! No, he wasn't. See – I have it here."

She scrabbled in a beach bag that was lying at her feet, and stood up triumphantly, holding a small pair of trunks.

"Then he can't have gone into the sea," said the young man. "Someone's sure to have seen a little boy fully clothed going into the water."

The thought calmed her.

"No, you're right. Thank heaven. But where can he be? My little baby all on his own, wandering about, lost. I can't bear to think of it."

Her eyes roamed the crowded, animated scene. Another possibility presented itself and she turned back to him.

"But perhaps he isn't on his own? Perhaps someone has taken him. Some woman baby–snatcher. You read of things like that. Or worse – some man. Dear heaven, what shall I do?"

And again she called down the beach: "Danny! Danny!"

"Calm," said the young man. "Keep calm, Mrs Weiss. We'll walk together along the sands, and if we don't find him we'll ask the lifeguard to make an announcement. But we'll find him, Mrs Weiss, never fear."

The woman seemed comforted. She looked up as if seeing him for the first time.

"You're so kind, Mr... There, I don't even know your name."

"I'm Uri Segal," said the young man. "Call me Uri. Now let's get started. We'll walk together. I'll look to the left, you look to the right."

Side by side the two of them ploughed their way through the sand, the young man with the towel, the woman with the beach bag – the woman calling "Danny! Danny!" from time to time, the young man concentrating on isolating a tiny sole figure from among the hundreds all around.

By three o'clock they had scoured the beach, the lifeguard had made a fruitless announcement, and the two of them were back close to their point of departure.

"I'm not sure there's much more I can do, Mrs Weiss," said Uri. "Shouldn't we contact your husband?"

The woman's grasp on her self–control seemed increasingly precarious. She looked at him vaguely.

"My husband?"

"Danny's father," said Uri. "Where is he?"

"Oh, I'm quite alone," said Mrs Weiss. "There's only me and Danny. You're not going to leave me now, are you, Uri? What shall I do?"

"There's only one thing left," said Uri. "We'll have to contact the police. Someone could have found Danny wandering on the promenade, or even in the town, and taken him to a police station."

"Yes, yes."

She grasped at the idea.

"He may be waiting for me now, waiting for his Mummy to come and find him – his wicked, wicked Mummy, who let him wander off on his own."

Again she was overcome with a fit of weeping.

"How could I have done it? How?"

Together they made their way to a street telephone. Mrs Weiss, a forlorn figure, stood aimlessly clutching her beach bag as Uri contacted the central police station at the far end of Dizengoff.

"I've got a distraught mother at my side. Her little boy has disappeared somewhere on the beach. We've searched as best we can; the lifeguard has broadcast an appeal. Nothing. Have you any news of a little boy being found?"

"You aren't the boy's father, I take it," said the desk sergeant.

"No, I'm not the father. I simply offered to help."

"And what is the child's name? And the mother's? And yours?"

Increasingly impatient with the calmly methodical policeman, Uri supplied the necessary information. The desk sergeant thought it advisable for them to come down to the station.

"In the meantime I'll be making a few enquiries – hospitals and so on. Get over here as soon as you can."

The woman stood by listlessly as Uri hailed a taxi, and she allowed him to usher her into the rear seat. As the car pulled away from the kerb, however, a sudden change of mood seemed to affect her. The apathy that had succeeded her previous bursts of hysteria fell away. In its place she became voluble, as if she felt an urgent need to explain herself precisely to the young man who had befriended her.

"How we yearned for that child. He was a long time in coming, you see, and we got frightened that there was something wrong – with one or other of us. You understand?"

She peered round into his face. Uri nodded.

"You can only comprehend the agony of yearning for a child if you have lived through it. Month after month, the prayers, the hopes, the disappointment. Month after month. The doctors, the prescriptions, the suggestions. Month after month. But when the months turn into years, and hope continues to turn into despair – then come the recriminations. Which one of us is being punished? And why? What have I done? What have you done? Month after month, year after year. Imagine what that does to a human being. And then – picture it, Uri. The same faint glimmer of hope as last month, as the month before – but this time the glimmer is not extinguished like a spark in the dying embers of a fire. This time the glimmer remains, grows stronger. You dare not let yourself believe it. You present yourself to your doctor in fear, in trembling. You take the tests. You wait for the verdict. Uri, can you possibly begin to understand what such a woman feels when she learns that the everyday miracle, so commonplace for so many, has at last occurred for her? And can you understand with what love, what adoration, that child is received?"

Suddenly, as if the release of words marked also the release of pent–up emotion, she burst again into a fit of crying.

"Oh my darling, darling baby. Where are you?"

The main Tel Aviv police station was comparatively calm for a July afternoon. The desk sergeant looked up as they approached,

"Ah yes, the missing child. You'll be Mrs Weiss."

"Have you any news?" she said.

"We've had a phone call," said the sergeant.

Mrs Weiss clasped her hands.

"Thank God. Thank God."

"…but I'm afraid," he went on, "there's nothing very definite."

"Not definite?" said Uri. "What do you mean?"

"A man rang just after I finished speaking to you."

"A man?" Uri was puzzled. "Did he say who he was?"

The policeman shook his head.

"Well, what did he say? Is it a kidnap? Will there be a demand for ransom?"

"All he said," said the desk sergeant, a grizzled man of unshakeable imperturbability, "was: 'Have you had a report of a missing child?'

When I said: 'Yes, the mother's just on her way to the station, ' he rang off."

"That's very strange," said Uri.

A man approached them from behind and stood in front of the desk. Uri glanced at him. Cool grey suit, neat beard. Mrs Weiss caught sight of him. Her face lit up.

"Dr Tannenbaum! What on earth are you doing here?"

"Hullo, Mrs Weiss," said the newcomer. "I was worried about you. You know I worry about you a lot."

Mrs Weiss's face was suffused with a great smile.

"Dear Dr Tannenbaum. You are so good to me."

The desk sergeant laid down his pen.

"I take it you know this lady, sir."

"Mrs Weiss and I are very well acquainted, sergeant," said Dr Tannenbaum.

He drew a paper out of his pocket and presented it across the desk.

"If you glance through this document, you'll see it certifies that Mrs Esther Weiss is a long–stay patient in the Eshkol Psychiatric Hospital, to which I have the honour to be consultant psychiatrist."

The policeman studied the paper carefully, before folding it and returning it.

"Yes, this seems in order."

"Poor Mrs Weiss does have a tendency to wander, from time to time," said Dr Tannenbaum.

"Well, doctor," said the desk sergeant, "and what am I to enter on this report? I take it there is no little boy?"

"Oh, there was," said the doctor, "twenty years ago. At the very end of the war, in Europe. Mrs Weiss was in one of the concentration camps with her son. They were picked up in '42, but she managed to keep her little boy with her. Then, with only a few weeks to liberation, they were separated. She was force–marched to somewhere further inside Germany; the child was kept in the original camp. She never saw her son again. After the end of the war she eventually found her way to Israel, but the shock of it all had unhinged her mind. For twenty years she has been searching for the son she so yearned for, and who was snatched away from her. Sometimes she prowls round the grounds of the hospital at night carrying a child's coat and calling for him; sometimes she goes to the nearest town and walks the streets. On occasion she gets further afield – like today."

"Poor woman," murmured Uri, for he had a very kind heart.

The doctor took her gently by the arm.

"Such beautiful blue eyes," said Mrs Weiss.

As he led her away, she looked Uri full in the face.

"Just like yours."

Uri was taken up with the woman's sad story.

"Still looking for her lost child," he said to the policeman. "After all that time."

"You still here?" said the sergeant. "What are you waiting for?"

"A happy ending?" said Uri. "Please – take a look at those particulars you took down so carefully. See what you have about me."

"Uri Segal," read out the sergeant. "Aged 24. That's right, isn't it?"

"As far as it goes," said Uri. "Yes, I'm 24, more or less. And yes, I'm known as Uri Segal. But there's more to it. You see, I came to Israel as a very young boy in a group of orphan children, and I grew up in a children's village. They told me that I came without papers or belongings of any sort. I didn't say a word for nearly six months. So they made up a name for me – it's as good as any other – and they guessed my age. So yes, for all practical purposes I'm Uri Segal, aged 24. But – and this is the incredible, the fantastic possibility – couldn't I just as well be Danny Weiss, little Danny lost at the age of four in 1945, sought for ever since and, by a chance in a million, found twenty years later by his own mother on the beach at Tel Aviv?"

You know what they say about the sea–front at Tel Aviv. Walk along it often enough, and you're bound to meet everyone you've ever known.

*

During August and September 1987 Israel was not at ease with itself. I filed two pieces for *The Spectator* under my Edmund Owen by-line. The first dealt exclusively with the *débacle* leading to the cancellation of the prestigious Israeli aircraft, the Lavi. In the second, "Holy Rows and Warplanes", I tried to paint the picture for a UK reader of the two major issues that were dominating the country at the time – not only the highly political, though evanescent, Lavi issue, but a religious problem that continues to vex the nation to this day. This article was published in *The Spectator* of 12 September 1987.

# THE LAVI DOWN THE DRAIN

The office of Israel's State Comptroller is a phenomenon of public administration that other advanced Western democracies might take a close look at. They would probably reject the idea for themselves because, like many another institution that is fine for others, it would prove a trifle uncomfortable to transplant. In Israel, the office holder is a sort of self-motivating national Ombudsman on the grand scale, a considerably more red-blooded animal than our own National Audit Officer – even the reconstituted version.

The State Comptroller has been a feature of Israel's public life for 37 of the State's 39 years. With a free-ranging brief to oversee the whole of Israeli public affairs, and to report annually to the nation, State Comptrollers have not on the whole been timid men. Ya'akov Maltz, the present holder of the office, is proving himself one of the most fearless. In June he attached to his customary catalogue of mismanagement and financial jiggery-pokery, a special report on the Lavi project of so searing an honesty that the Government was forced to the agonising reappraisal that has this week resulted in the aborting of the programme.

Maltz's report traced a history of botched and ill-founded Government decisions stretching across more than a decade. Linked to this series of politically expedient, but economically unjustified, activity is a pattern – familiar in prestige projects elsewhere than in Israel – of ever-escalating costs, to the point where any rationale for continuation turned on increasingly speculative projections of possible future benefits,

The Lavi story goes back to 1974, when Israel Aircraft Industries had completed development of the Kfir fighter based on the French Mirage. It put in a report to the Government recommending that a start be made quickly on its successor. A decision in favour was first made in February 1980 by then defense minister Ezer Weizman, but according to the Comptroller it was taken without sufficient regard to the project's economic viability. In particular, military top brass would have preferred upgrading the Kfir, a $2bn project in its own right, but that alternative was not even considered. Nor was the option of producing an American design, notably the F-16C jet, in Israel – the decision that was finally taken this week, 7½ years later. Worse, Comptroller Maltz could find no evidence of detailed consideration of the Levi's projected capabilities, development risks or its implications for employment, technology and exports.

Since the project was to be largely funded through the American military aid programme, Washington appointed a team to work alongside Israeli experts. "Cooperation within the Israeli team, and between it and the American team, was faulty," reported the Comptroller, adding that at one time the Americans were even being refused leave to examine the Levi plans.

All this and much more, although refuted point by point by the Government shortly after the Comptroller's report appeared, was examined in detail by the Knesset State Control Committee. In evidence provided to the committee by the State Comptroller's office, it became clear that some of the crucial decisions leading to the parlous financial state of the project which resulted in its collapse were taken by Menachem Begin at a time when he was both Premier and defense minister.

A key date was May 29th 1981. Three men met Begin on that day – then finance minister, Yoram Aridor, Treasury director-general, Ezra Sadan, and deputy defense minister, Mordechai Zipori. All stressed that essential cost-benefit and cost-effectiveness assessments had not taken place, and laid particular emphasis on the lack of economic analysis of the proposal to install a far heavier US-made engine – the PW 1120 –than originally envisaged.

Begin swept all objections aside. There had been too much shilly-shallying, and he was minded to take the decision. He took it. Once taken, it should have been referred to the Ministerial Defense Committee. According to the Comptroller, it was not.

The Lavi, which symbolised Israel's state-of-the-art military technology, was enormously popular with the Israeli public, A few weeks ago Israel Aircraft Industries' workers signed an agreement with management to dock one day's pay a month to, help cut costs – and this despite IAI's known intention to sack some 1000 workers. This agreement might have added $12m to the savings already projected in the current year, but it would not have made much practical difference to the outcome.

The Lavi issue cut across party lines. Both Likud Premier Yitzhak Shamir and his Labour deputy, Shimon Peres, supported the project's continuance; the defense minister, Yotzhak Rabin, and finance minister, Moshe Nissim wanted it scrapped, especially since it had become clear that Washington would not have sanctioned the use of its military aid to fund further development. It could only have been continued at the cost of an open-ended commitment on the country's already massive national debt.

The *coup de grace* became inevitable when George Shultz, US Secretary of State, wrote to a selection of Israel's ministers. Considering it was largely US dollars going down the plughole, his was the decisive – though absent – voice inside the Cabinet room at the Knesset when the die was finally cast.

*

# HOLY ROWS AND WARPLANES

*Jerusalem*

It's been a long, hot summer, and political protest has taken to the streets. Mass demonstrations are the order of the day. Marvellous for hands–on training of police recruits in crowd control, no doubt, but it is a bit much when the *Jerusalem Post* parades as its main feature 'What to do when the tear gas flies'.

None of the unrest, let it be said, is connected with the Palestinian problem. The two issues that have suddenly come to the boil are quintessentially domestic. One is all about the extent to which the majority of the Israeli population – easy–going, most of them, as regards religious observance – are prepared to be dictated to by the hard–line ultra–orthodox.

For the seventh weekend in a row, religious militants have set up protest demonstrations in the city. Two weeks ago they paraded at 18 major intersections; last Friday night they appeared at 24. The bearded, black–coated demonstrators are violently opposed to infringement of the Sabbath in general, and to the showing of films on the Sabbath in particular. Throwing bottles and rocks at the police and at passing vehicles (and incidentally breaking the Sabbath themselves with a vengeance), the demonstrators were repeatedly charged by the helmeted policemen, who used water cannon and tear gas to disperse the mob. The next day the media reported that all the cinemas on Friday night had been packed solid – a secular demonstration of a sort, one supposes.

Water cannon and tear gas have been much in evidence in Israel's other major political row. A week after the wafer–thin cabinet decision (12–11) to scrap the Lavi aircraft project, the political repercussions still rumble on, erupting at a moment's notice into mass demonstrations by workers understandably fearful for their jobs.

The Lavi aircraft had become in the public perception a symbol of Israel's status as an advanced technological nation. But the recent report by the state comptroller (a sort of free–ranging public ombudsman) clearly showed up the muddled thinking and lack of adequate cost-benefit analysis that preceded the decision, taken by Menachem Begin in 1981, to go ahead with the multi–billion dollar project.

Inevitably, unforeseen problems emerged and costs escalated. The original plan had been to build 300 planes. By the start of 1985 that had been scaled down to 210 – at a cost estimated at 33 per cent more than buying American F–16s off the shelf, or ten per cent more than building F–16s in Israel. By the time the cabinet met to agonise over the project a fortnight ago, the plan was to build only 100 planes, though of course at an enormously increased unit cost.

Hopes of recouping the Lavi's development costs by way of sales were always illusory. Even the Kfir – Israel Aircraft Industry's highly successful predecessor to the Lavi – grossed only $1 billion export sales as against its $2.5 billion development costs. The Lavi was finally calculated to come in at some $3.5 billion, of which at least $1.5 billion – and possibly as much as $2 billion – has already been spent.

Where did the money come from? From the US military aid budget, most of it. It was not only when Washington indicated that it was not prepared to continue funding the development of the Lavi that harder–headed elements in the government (notably finance minister Moshe Nissim), the opposition and the military felt free to come out openly against the project. If Israel were to shoulder the remainder of the development costs itself, Nissim foresaw a huge increase in the national deficit, undoing the substantial economic gains of the past two years. Neither did the defense minister nor the military chiefs relish the thought of the heavy drain on their budgets that would result. In any case, there had always been a strong feeling in military circles that the correct decision right at the start would have been to go for the F–16.

Hence the cabinet decision, albeit by a whisker, to scrap, and the mass demonstrations of Israel Aircraft Industry workers day after day ever since. Barricaded roads, burned tyres, even the blocking of a runway at Ben Gurion Airport, culminated on Sunday with a mass rally of all 20,000 IAI workers near the Prime Minister's Office where the cabinet were discussing the implications of their decision.

Some 5,000 IAI workers were directly employed in producing the Lavi. Defense minister Yitzhak Rabin has instructed the company to dismiss 3,000. The rest, IAI has been led to understand, can be employed on new military projects and perhaps even on some of the technologically advanced projects initially developed for the Lavi which could be used in other weapons systems.

What senior military and aviation industry people are really hoping for, though, is practical help from Washington. For example, the idea is abroad that IAI might continue the research and development programme on the Lavi's advanced avionic technology. The aim would be to use it in the F–16C fighter–bomber, which is to be co–produced with the US in Israel, as well as in a next–generation F–16 (already codenamed Agile Falcon), and even in the highly secret ATF – the Advanced Tactical Fighter – the new–generation F–15 currently being developed by the Americans for the 1990s.

Agile Falcon is designed to be more manoeuvrable than the F–16, to have a larger engine and to carry more weapons. At the moment, though, it is on General Dynamics' drawing–board. Their proposal, currently frozen with the USAF, is for development and production to be shared by the US–European consortium involved in co–producing the F–16 at present. Now Israel hopes to be admitted to the producers' club, but all turns on whether the project itself is ultimately approved.

As for the ATF, it would take a great deal to assure Israel a slice of that action. At present US rules forbid any foreign involvement – understandably, since at the heart of the ATF project is state–of–the–art stealth technology, or in other words the capacity to out-manoeuvre enemy radar.

More likely options for Caspar Weinberger to consider would be a variety of ways of increasing US procurement of Israeli military goods and services. In particular, the Arrow Anti Tactical Ballistic Missile (ATBM) is an advanced project within sight of deployment and one, moreover, that is defined as a tactical weapon. It would not affect any US–USSR agreement on intermediate or short–range missiles.

Unfortunately neither this, nor the range of other potentially attractive US contracts for military procurement that might be on offer for Israel, would do much to placate IAI or the Lavi workers. They might well exacerbate the domestic problem. The mere idea that work might be transferred from Rafael, the Armaments Development Agency, to IAI has been enough to raise workers' hackles. Warning shots are already being fired in what could well be a new skirmish in the Lavi battle.

*The Spectator*

*14 September 1987*

*

In addition to Israel's internal political disputes during that long, hot summer of 1987, two great public show trials dominated the domestic agenda – that of Ivan Demjanjuk, accused of being Ivan the Terrible of the Treblinka death camp; and that of Mordechai Vanunu, snatched from Europe to stand trial in Israel accused of espionage.

# TRYING TIMES

*Jerusalem*

Poised between the Hilton Hotel and the central bus station – betwixt heaven and hell, as 'twere – Jerusalem's *Binyanei Ha'Oomah*, a gaunt conference centre–cum–cinema, has for the past six months provided the setting for a public spectacle on a par with the Roman Games.

Before the Demjanjuk hearings began last February, pundits doubted whether the Israeli public would evince any great interest. The war was 40 long years away, Demjanjuk was no Eichmann, and the numbers of those with direct experience of the Holocaust were rapidly diminishing.

No greater miscalculation could have been made. Within days the trial had become the focus of public attention. Early each morning queues of people intent on attending the day's drama snake round the building, parties of schoolchildren are regularly bussed in to experience a personal link with far–off events that would otherwise remain unreal, and the proceedings are broadcast live and continuously on the radio.

The trial turns on a question of identification. Is the man in the dock – a car industry worker of Ukrainian extract called Ivan Demjanjuk from Cleveland, Ohio, father of three – the brutal guard known as Ivan the Terrible in the Treblinka death camp, where some 800,000 Jews were gassed to death in 1942 and 1943?

The testimony has been long and, inevitably, harrowing. There have also been some oddly disturbing moments – such as the occasion when Demjanjuk suddenly proffered his hand to prosecution witness Eliyahu Rosenburg who, still shaken from reliving horrendous events, reacted to the overture with revulsion and rage. Or Demjanjuk blowing kisses to the public. Or the constant disagreements between the prisoner and his counsel, Mark O'Connor, which culminated in Demjanjuk dismissing him and a new defense leader, Yoram Shaftal, taking over.

Nothing, however, has so far equalled the latest bizarre twist.

It all started when two expert witnesses for the defense , specially flown in from the States, took the stand. Edna Robertson is a documents expert and president of WADE – the World Association of Document Examiners. A key document in the prosecution case is a Trawniki camp identification card issued to a John Demjanjuk (Trawniki was an SS camp used to train concentration camp guards).

The card carries a photograph partly overprinted with two circular rubber stamps. Robertson testified that the card was a forgery, that the parts of the rubber stamp on the photograph did not match those on the card, and that the signature on the card was not in Demjanjuk's handwriting.

Cross examination was relentless, in the classic tradition of the British judicial system to which Israel still largely clings. Step by step Michael Shaked, leader for the prosecution, forced Robertson back from her initial position, slowly undermining her professional standing by uncovering the far from scientific approach she had adopted in her examination of the crucial evidence. Admission after admission was wrung from the reluctant witness, as her earlier testimony crumbled. No, she had not chemically tested a stain on the ID card; no, she had not considered that iron in the ink could have caused a rust stain; yes, she had failed to order a thin–layer-chromatology test.

Her insistence that none of these things mattered was, however, too much for the judges. One of them declared, not unreasonably, that the court's concept was that experts should know their disciplines.

"You want to convince us that a little knowledge of inks, of paper and of instruments is sufficient."

Shaked's final *coup de théâtre* was admittedly more in the tradition of Perry Mason than Marshall Hall. He set up in the courtroom a visual spectral comparator (VCS), borrowed from the police laboratory. The VCS distinguishes different inks by measuring their varying luminescence. A series of video screens linked to the instrument were positioned strategically around the court.

Back in Panama City, Florida, Edna Robertson had used a VCS to reach her conclusion that the Trawniki ID card was a forgery. She had found that the ink on that part of the circular stamp covering the photograph luminesced differently from what was apparently the remainder. When Shaked repeated the experiment in the court, the machine at first indicated precisely the same luminescence for both parts of the stamp.

"This is not what I saw when I performed my test," said Robertson.

After several further attempts, she claimed there was a difference.

"This is not the brilliant contrast I observed earlier," she said. "It fades in and out... but I can see a dimmer version of the difference."

At that point Shaked produced Demjanjuk's 1947 driver's licence, whose authenticity is not in doubt. When tested in the VCS, variations in luminescence between part of a rubber stamp printed on a photograph and part printed on the card showed up.

A devastating day for Robertson ended with Shaked asking:

"In chemistry, what does C stand for?"

Robertson: "I am not a chemist."

Shaked: "If you look at a molecular chart, do you know what it is about?"

Robertson: "No."

Shaked: "So how do you testify in a court about ink, if you don't know its chemical composition?"

Robertson: "I have taken specialised courses on paper and on ink."

A discomforted president of WADE retired from the witness stand to be replaced by an acolyte. Anita Pritchard, a member of WADE, studied grapho–analysis and art and is the author of "Identifying Faces from Handwriting." She specialises in the rather dubious discipline of linking personality traits to facial features. A series of photo—montages of the faces of male models briefly enlivened the proceedings, while Pritchard attempted to disprove earlier efforts by prosecution experts to match the photo on the Trawniki ID card with known photographs of Demjanjuk.

Finally one of the Judges, Dalia Dorner, clearly unmoved by the male models, asked Pritchard how all this was accepted in the scientific community.

Pritchard: "Facial montages are accepted, but I don't know how much they apply to forensic cases. My experience is in psychology."

Anita Pritchard's testimony ended at 6 pm on Wednesday. She spent Thursday in her room at the American Colony Hotel in East Jerusalem, writing letters to her husband, her mother and the defense lawyers. Late in the afternoon she slit her wrists and swallowed more than 50 tablets containing a variety of medicinal drugs.

The suicide attempt was discovered at 8 pm and she was rushed to the Bikur Holim hospital. "She said she didn't want to live," the duty doctor is reported as saying. "She didn't want us to help her. She pulled out the intravenous tubes."

Nonetheless she was sufficiently recovered after 48 hours to fly back to the States.

On that high note the trial went into recess until September 7th. Just as well, really, because there can be too much of a good thing and Sunday, August 30th, saw the start of Israel's second great legal drama – the trial of Mordechai Vanunu for espionage.

The hearing opened with the case for the prosecution and representations on the admissibility of the evidence. The most elaborate precautions were taken to ensure that not a whisper of what passed in the courtroom reached the public. But one development could not be withheld. Three days after the trial began, one of the three judges, Zvi Tal – also, as it happens, a member of the judicial panel in the Demjanjuk hearing – suffered a heart attack. Fortunately the Vanunu trial was planned in any case to go into immediate recess until mid–

October, which it did. The resumption of the Demjanjuk trial was postponed until early November at the earliest.

Both sets of defense counsel have been putting their respective recesses to good use. The Vanunu team has successfully pressed for a series of privileges for their incarcerated client, who can now, by order of the Jerusalem District Court, send tape–recorded messages to his American girl–friend, Judy Zimmet, and listen to a radio without earphones (but he cannot use the phone, communicate with his priest, or have food brought in from outside). Word is that Amnesty International are on the scene. We shall see.

The Demjanjuk defense has had foremost British documents expert, Dr Julius Grant, flown in to re–examine the Trawniki camp card and, with the agreement of the court, called in yet two more experts.

Meanwhile, all Israel is poised for a resumption of what is now due to become a two–ring circus.

\*

By late-1987, the forthcoming 40<sup>th</sup> anniversary of Israel's Declaration of Independence was casting its shadow before it. I wrote this (unpublished) piece for *The Spectator*.

## ISRAEL'S ELGIN MARBLES

*Jerusalem*

Ring out the old, ring in the new, and a happy 5748 to you. If that seems a somewhat space–age New Year salutation, be assured that Thursday 24<sup>th</sup> September 1987 does indeed coincide with the lst of Tishri 5748 in the Hebrew calendar, and that the whole of Israel has been celebrating its Rosh Hashana with a public holiday, religious services, and a good deal of eating, drinking and celebration.

The reason why the Jewish New Year is 5748 is, as Shakespeare has it somewhere, a pretty reason, all bound up with cycles of the moon and a belief, somewhere around the eighth century AD, that the world had been brought into being some 3.000 years previously. It was on that conception that the sequential numbering of years in the Hebrew lunar calendar began.

Let that not detain us. Let us rather, in accordance with time—honoured custom, speculate on what the new year will bring.

In this instance the crystal ball is a good deal less cloudy than usual. This is because 5748 will mark Israel's 40th anniversary, and the whole year has been set aside to celebrate the occasion (the fact that it will also be election year has been conveniently forgotten for the moment). A massive list of events has been drawn up by a committee that has been hard at work for months, a body whose importance is reflected in its budget of £7 million.

The centre—piece of the year will be Independence Day itself. In the Hebrew calendar this is always the 5th of Iyar. However, the 5th of Iyar in the year 5708 was the 14th May 1948, while the 5th of Iyar in 5748 will be the 22nd April 1988. Nobody understands exactly why, except that it's all bound up with cycles of the moon.

Why make such a fuss of a 40th anniversary – not a particularly significant one, as Yitzhak Navon, chairman of the Parliamentary Symbols and Ceremonies Committee, remarked last week when displaying the forthcoming goodies to assembled foreign journalists. The reason is essentially the same as that which moved us to make much in 1985 of the 40th anniversary of the ending of the war. Many of the people directly involved might not be around if celebrations are postponed until the Golden Jubilee.

These forthcoming events were inaugurated at a special ceremony on Sunday attended, *inter alia*, by the only surviving member of the team that drafted Israel's Declaration of Independence. Also present, and why not, was the secretary who typed its first English version.

46

Britain is, of course, intimately bound up in the occasion. Comparisons may be odious, but the drafting of the American and the Israeli Declarations of Independence do have in common the fact that Britain was – to put it no more strongly – very much in the minds of both sets of draftsmen.

Several reconstructions of historical occasions are a feature of the planned catalogue of events. One such will be the turning back in Haifa Bay of the "Exodus" and its shipload of illegal immigrants – a reminder of an unhappy time when Britain was struggling with an intractable problem that is still, 40 years on, not in sight of solution. Not only historical pageants, but arts festivals, parades, conventions, exhibitions are all in active preparation – a veritable cornucopia of celebration. One wonders if the Israeli appetite for public spectacle might not have become somewhat jaded by the time 5749 dawns.

Speaking of exhibitions, one of the most important is planned for the Knesset – Israel's Parliament. Independence Day itself, the 5th of Iyar (which, for argument's sake, let us assume will be the 22nd April according to the cycles of the moon), has been chosen, to unveil a unique display of the most important documents in the state's history. But the most important document of all, the very foundation stone of the state, is not in Israel's possession. I refer, of course, to the Balfour Declaration in which, on 2nd November 1917, His Majesty's Government declared that it viewed "with favour the establishment in Palestine of a national home for the Jewish people."

And that is why Yehuda Avner, Israel's ambassador to the Court of St James, will shortly be making representations to that universal guardian of other people's national treasures, the British Museum, for a loan of the original for at least a cycle or two of the moon. The cost of transportation would not, unlike some other national treasures lodged under the same roof, be a problem.

\*

The background to, and the events surrounding, Israel's 40th birthday in 1988 were inevitably reflected in the pieces that appeared at the time in "Edmund Owen's Israel" in the *Jewish Telegraph*.

# THE PASSING SCENE – 2

The bus from Tiberias labours more and more as it ascends the hills north of Lake Kinneret in great sweeping zig–zags. Eventually it decants its passengers in a town of extraordinary character, nestling away up in the mountains. Safed (pronounced S'fat) is so high it actually dominates the heights of Lebanon which lie only a few miles off to the north and west.

I wandered into the synagogue quarter of the old city, just off Kikar Ha'Meginim. Safed has a long history as a religious centre, and is especially associated with the development of the mystic study of the Caballah. Its religious connections are marked by the number of ancient and beautiful synagogues.

I pushed open the door of one and ventured into the dim interior. I had chanced upon the mediaeval Sephardi Ha'Ari shool. An elderly member of the congregation, unseen at first in the shadows, emerged and insisted on showing off the building.

"See that wall outside – that's a sort of barricade. Can't you see – the synagogue is built like a fortress. During the 1948 war, this was the Hagana headquarters."

I oo'ed and ah'ed, and he rewarded me by giving detailed directions to the monument to the fallen in the 1948 War of Independence. Safed was the scene of fierce battles during the Arab attack on the newly born State of Israel, and in this town the 40th anniversary is being remembered as a time of special significance.

I followed the old man's instructions, and came to the beautiful park which has been created, and lovingly maintained, on the northern edge of the town.

One stands on grass, under trees, and looks out upon a wonderful view that stretches towards Lebanon. At a high spot stands an impressive piece of sculpture as a memorial to those who fought and died to ensure that Israel was not strangled at birth. The 40th anniversary is, however, the best of all memorials to their sacrifice.

I strolled down from the park through Safed's High Street, Rehov Yerushalayim, (where, incidentally, I took in one of the best falafels I'd enjoyed in a long time) and found my way to the town's other outstanding attraction – Kiryat Ha'tzayarim.

Safed is a notable centre for Israel's artists, and the artists' quarter is filled with studios and craftsmen's workshops, set in an enchanting area of old houses and cobbled alleys. Half of its charm lies in the variety of multi-coloured signs, painted front doors and metal lampshades, that give a unique character to the place.

Right in the centre sits a public gallery where the work of the artists and craftsmen of Sated are on exhibition. Painting, leather and metal work, printing (Safed is a great printing centre), glass, jewellery, sculpture – all this and more are on permanent display.

One thing. If you elect to visit Safed from a base in Jerusalem or Tel Aviv, remember the last buses from Tiberias leave unexpectedly early. Be sure to get back in good time. Be warned!

\*

Even in this anguished and disrupted 40th Anniversary year – with tensions between Arab and Jew high and mass media comment in the outside world focussed on the violence – life goes on.

With my own eyes I see Arab workmen in Bet Ha'Kerem stop, untold prayer mats and quite unconcernedly undertake midday worship, while Jewish mothers wheel their children past on their way from the Jerusalem Baby Home (a WIZO project incidentally).

I can vouch for keffiyeh–wrapped Arab citizens mingling with the crowds of Jewish shoppers in Hamashbir's – Jerusalem's main department store – without a backward glance from either of the parties. Middle–class Arab ladies shop down Ben–Yehuda, side by side with middle-class Jewish ladies and the tourists.

Of course none of this affects the serious and long-standing differences between Jew and Arab, which must be resolved. But to me it does represent a sign that the idea of peaceful co–existence is more than a pipe–dream. It is actually being lived, day by day, despite the turmoil. If it can persist even in present troubles, it is a hardy plant and must be nurtured.

\*

Driving up from Jerusalem to Zichron Ya'akov, I was struck by how fertile the coastal plain is. The cultivated areas spread, green and luscious, on either side of the main highway all the 80 miles or so of the way – orange groves, banana plantations, apples, apricots, lemons, grapefruit, artichokes, dates, figs... mile after mile. Amazing to think that only 100 years ago most of the area was sand, scrub or swamp.

The passing of a century is very much in evidence in Zichron Ya'akov, which was founded by the Baron Edmond de Rothschild in 1885. And the town – one of the earliest of the successful Zionist ventures – is only just getting over its own centenary celebrations.

Every now and then, following that, some other institution in the town has its own centenary. Thus, the Ashkenazi synagogue had its own 100th birthday only last year, while the local high school celebrates its centenary this year.

The Ashkenazi shool in Zichron is very much home from home as far as the services are concerned. The differences are in the externals.

For example, it takes no less than 21 wall-mounted electric fans, all on the move backwards and forwards, and most of the 30 windows flung open, to keep a reasonably–filled synagogue reasonably comfortable.

I was delighted to be given an aliyah, and to be able to offer a small donation to help the redecoration programme that is currently under way.

Zichron was founded as an agricultural settlement, but very short-ly afterwards Baron de Rothschild, a Frenchman, decided to import vines and try wine production. Hence the world famous Carmel winery, the largest kosher wine producer in the world. I was shown over the large modernised facilities, and was particularly impressed with the automated bottling machinery that takes over the mecha-nism of packaging, once the miracle of producing nectar from bunch-es of grapes has been achieved.

Zichron Ya'akov is perched on top of a hill. From various van-tage points around the town you can see, not only the huge areas of cultivation that spread around it, but also a great stretch composed of artificial lakes – fish farms engaged in the scientific cultivation of carp and other delicacies for the home market and for export. Not so far away, beyond the fish farms, lies the blue Mediterranean, only about 10 miles distant.

*

Driving through the West Bank, these days, one cannot have the same carefree attitude of even a couple of years back. Political realities have brought the inherent problems of the area into sharper focus.

Half–way between Jerusalem and Hebron, well into the West Bank in the territory of Judea, lies the Gush Etzion – a group of Orthodox settlements and moshavim (communal farms).

On the way to friends in Moshav Elazar, I visited the yeshuv, or township, of Alon Shevut. The area was Jewish–owned well before 1948, but when the settlers returned after the 1947 war, the only remnant of all their previous extensive planting was a solitary oak tree. So they renamed the place Alon Shevut (the Return to the Oak Tree). And there the oak still flourishes, as you drive through the guarded entrance.

I went on a tour of the yeshuv, and could immediately see why the place was re-settled so quickly. It is clearly of vital strategic importance. From a special terrace which is equipped with a powerful pair of fixed binoculars on a stand and a panoramic guide beautifully made of metal, you can command a vast tract of country, including the southern suburbs of Jerusalem.

Moshav Elazar, a short distance away, one also enters past a guard post. The high mesh fence topped by barbed wire which surrounds the outer perimeter of the moshav, and the small army camp on the other side of the road, are a grim reminder of the uneasy political situation, which can erupt at any time into violence.

Yet, of course, life goes on in the Gush day to day with every appearance of normality. Two buses an hour run regularly to Jerusalem, the children go to school, the Bet Ha–Knesset has a minyan for sha-charit, mincha and ma'ariv every day, and in the nearby expanding township of Efrat Arab workmen are everywhere, helping to build the many new houses that are springing up.

*

It was the whole atmosphere of the 40th Anniversary, and the memories it evoked of the period surrounding the historic declaration of 14 May 1948, that suddenly sparked the idea of a short story. I thought of those frenetic months that followed the end of the Second World War, when Jews released from the camps, but with no homes, no families – "displaced persons" in the jargon of the times – were desperate to reach Palestine, while the British, responsible for the civil administration and struggling to control an increasingly uncontrollable situation, were equally desperate to keep them out.

# VENGEANCE

The children were intrigued by the naval museum that was half a ship. Ships and the sea were not things they had grown up with. The occasional visit to the Dead Sea was as far north as they usually ventured. They had been to the seaside at Tel Aviv so rarely that you could count the occasions on the fingers of one hand. No, our two grandchildren were children of the desert.

You see, when I came to settle in Israel late in 1949, it was way down south in the Negev that I started a small business, taking my Hebrew name from the most important town in the area. So it was as Avraham Ramon that I was shortly afterwards married to a girl I had known as a child in the old country.

Down south we made our life and brought up our son. He went to the Ben Gurion University of the Negev shortly after it was founded in 1969, and when he got married he settled close to us. And so our two grandchildren grew up knowing the ways of the desert, and our big family excitement was a day's outing to Beer-Sheva, the nearest city.

When our grandson, Eli, reached his twelfth birthday in 1985, I wanted to give him and his little sister, Shula, the biggest treat I could. A week's holiday in Haifa was something the children had never experienced – they'd never been so far north before in their lives. I booked rooms in a luxury hotel, and our plan was to visit all the places of interest in the city – the port, the zoo, Elijah's cave – and then explore the rest of the area by car.

It was on the second morning of our holiday that my two grandchildren and I, walking up a steep side-road that ran at an acute angle from the main coast road, came across the odd–looking building with a rather unusual sign outside.

"What do those words mean, Grandpa?" asked Eli.

I spelled them out for him.

" 'Illegal Immigration and Naval Museum.' "

"What's illegal immigration?" asked Shula.

"Now, thank God, nothing," I said. "Once upon a time it was the only way that Jews could get into Eretz Israel. It means coming in unlawfully."

Eli knew what I was talking about.

"It's all those stories you used to tell us about when you were young. Let's go in, Grandpa. Oh look, Shula – the museum's half a ship."

"Where?" asked Shula. "What do you mean?"

"Can't you see? Sitting out there behind the entrance – it's a ship."

"So it is," I said. "They must have brought an old ship up here, and made it into a sort of living story book. Look – there are two children climbing that ladder to the top deck."

"Come on, Shula," said Eli. "We can pretend we're sailors."

We walked in, and instantly the glare of the morning sun was transmuted into a dim, greenish light, and we stepped from the heat into air-conditioned comfort. As I bought the tickets, I asked the man at the desk the name of the ship that had been integrated into the museum.

Grizzled, bearded, he looked at me intently before pointing up at the ship's side.

"The *Af Al Pi Khen*," he said, "one of the vessels that used to bring illegal immigrants into the port of Haifa under the noses of the British. During the Mandate, of course. There's plenty to see – and there's a film show half-way round."

"Can we go and explore, grandpa?" asked Eli.

"Yes, off you go. I'll never keep pace with you. I'll just go round in my own time."

"I want to see the film show," said Shula.

Eli grabbed her hand.

"No, no. First we go round the boat."

And they raced away.

I turned to the man at the desk.

54

·"It seems like a very good place to bring children."

"Oh, kids like scrambling about the ship. For them it's an adventure. But the story we tell here – that's a different matter. That's no fairy tale."

"I know," I said.

"I was in the middle of it all," said the man.

"Is that how you came to work in the museum?"

"Partly. Yes, I was well qualified, I suppose. The Haganah, first in the '30s and then after the Second World War, and then a spell in the Israeli Navy. But by that time I was already searching for someone – someone I wanted to find very badly indeed. When I left the Navy I looked for a job where I could go on searching. This was ideal."

"Sounds intriguing," I said. "Who are you searching for?"

"You want to know? I'll tell you. But it's best if I tell you the whole story. This is a quiet time – we don't have many visitors in the morning. Have you got time for a chat?"

"Why not? The children seem happy enough."

I took a seat.

"Your grandchildren?" asked the man.

"That's right."

"Lovely children. You've been lucky."

He paused, as if seeking the best way to break into the narrative.

"Why am I searching?" he said. "It goes back to 1946, '47 – that time, you know, between the end of the Second World War and the founding of the State."

His words brought back memories.

"I know," I said.

The brilliant sunlight, so harsh outside, had been defeated by the blinds that covered the windows, and the glare had been attenuated into soft green unfocused light. The man sat against a wall, his face only half visible.

"Well, go on." I said.

"Where to begin? After the War who had time or patience with bureaucracy and politics? Our people, the pitiful remnants who had survived Hitler's camps, were still in camps – refugee camps – still suffering humiliation, degradation. And still yearning, as Jews had yearned for two thousand years, for Eretz Israel. But for them, at that time, it was the only possible haven. The situation was unbearable. We had to bring them in. We bought, borrowed, chartered, whatever vessels we could from wherever we could. We organised collections of our people from pick–up points in Europe. We brought them across the sea. We brought them to within sight of the land. And then we faced the British blockade.

"So we had to smuggle them in – or try to.

"Each vessel needed at least one experienced leader to organise the voyage, to shepherd the dispirited immigrants, to act as the link with the reception committee here in Israel. Sometimes more than one was assigned. The main Jewish defense bodies participated.

"I told you I'd been in the Haganah in the '30s. I was born in this country, but I knew Europe. I was an obvious shipment leader.

"It was in the autumn of 1947 that I was appointed leader for one particular voyage. Everything went smoothly at the European end. I had the passengers on board and we were about to set sail for Haifa, when I received instructions that a co–leader from the Palmach had been assigned.

"Now, this is important. The instructions came to me by radio, in the normal code being used at that time. I had no reason to question them. But I was uneasy from the beginning. I was even more uncertain when the man named in the message arrived on board shortly afterwards – tall, thin, fair–haired, blue–eyed and clearly a native German speaker. He looked like the archetypal Aryan – and he aroused in me the strongest possible antipathy. I felt from the first moment that I couldn't trust the man.

"Then he told me that he'd been assigned to the trip by the Palmach because he had to get over to Eretz Israel, and they thought I could do with some help.

" 'I've managed so far,' I told him. Then I tried to get some background from him. But he was strangely reluctant to tell me anything much.

" 'Where are you from?' I asked.

" 'Do you mean where was I born? Berlin.'

" 'No, where have you come from?'

" 'Oh, all over. American Zone, British Zone.'

"I persisted.

" 'Where did you spend the war?'

" 'In a fighting unit,' he told me, 'once I was old enough. I was shipped over to Palestine with a group of other kids in '39 when I was 13 – straight after my Barmitzvah. My parents stayed on in Germany – rounded up in '41. OK? End of interrogation?'

" 'Not quite,' I said. 'You said you've got to get to Eretz Israel. Why?'

" 'Not that it's any of your business,' he said, 'but I'm getting married.'

"That's when I exploded. Frustrated already by his obvious reluctance to account for himself, tense under the strain of dealing with hundreds of desperate people, this seemed like frivolity run riot.

" 'Getting married? You're getting married? What do you think this is – a pleasure cruise? We've gathered up a bunch of the most hopeless, down–trodden, maltreated human beings the world has ever seen; they're herded together on this leaky vessel In conditions that rival the worst of Hitler's camps – and you decide to use the occasion to meet your bride. What the hell are the Palmach thinking about?'

"The Palmach man tried to calm me down.

" 'Keep your hair on. I don't see what's so wrong. I've led refugee shipments in the past – I know what I'm doing. So what, if I'm married once we've landed? I haven't seen my fiancée for nearly a year anyway.'

" 'What's wrong.' I said, 'is that you've been assigned to this vessel. I don't need you – that's what's wrong.'

" 'Is that all?' he said. 'Then I'll keep out of your way.'

" 'No, it's not all. I don't know you – that's worse. Because that means I don't trust you. Right?'

" 'Couldn't be clearer,' he said. 'From now on I'm just one of the refugees – OK? – and you're sole leader. Or, as we Germans say, *der Fuehrer*. OK?'

The man at the desk paused, and looked across at me. I said nothing. I kept my eyes on his face as I waited to hear the rest of his story. After a moment he continued.

"But the way things worked out, I wasn't able to do without him. Those vessels – they had to be seen to be believed. Only hope kept some of them afloat – and then not always. On this trip, in addition to all our other difficulties, we'd had trouble with the radio from the start. Finally, when we'd hove to, just over the horizon from Haifa – out of sight of the British observers – it gave up. That was pretty disastrous. It meant we couldn't contact the reception committee, back on the mainland, waiting to organise the run Into shore and the disembarkation. So I just had to turn to the man from the Palmach.

" 'There's only one thing for it,' I said. 'You'll have to row for the shore and make contact with the reception committee.'

"He could scarcely believe his ears.

" 'Row for the shore?'

" 'That's what I said.'

" 'But we're 16 kilometres from the coast.'

" 'Even so. There's no other way.'

" 'The other way,' he said 'is to repair the radio.'

" 'Keep your helpful suggestions to yourself,' I told him. 'Do you think we haven't tried? You can't create spare parts out of thin air.'

" 'Are you sure you can't patch something up?'

I was on a short fuse.

" 'Are you questioning my judgment? I've gone into it with everyone on board who has the slightest knowledge of radio. Given a week – three days, even – we might get it going again. Might. But we haven't got the time. Every hour of daylight that we lie out here we run the risk of discovery by British spotter planes. Do you understand? I won't have these people exposed to one hour of danger more than is necessary. So you will set out at 5 p.m. today. You will have two hours of daylight and four of our precious night hours to row to the shore and make contact. Precisely six hours after you have left, at 11 p.m., we will begin to edge towards the coast. I expect to see the current Haganah welcoming message by Morse lamp from the top of Mount Carmel during the night – in good time for us to get to the beach and disembark our passengers. Now, is that all understood?'

" 'Received and understood, captain' he said, with mock civility. 'Now, when you say the current Haganah message...?'

" 'Yes?'

" 'Look,' he said, 'I'm Palmach. How do I know the current Haganah code?'

I could scarcely believe what I was hearing.

" 'Are you telling me that you were sent as co–leader on this trip without being told the coded reception message?'

'Strange as it may seem.'

"This put the seal on my innate suspicion of the man – the suspicion I'd nurtured from the start.

" 'Well,' I said, 'if they didn't trust you with it, neither will I. It's bad enough that I have to place the success of this whole venture in your hands. I only wish one of the others on board had the strength to row that boat. Anyone, I'd prefer – anyone.'

" 'Be reasonable,' he said. 'You have to send me – there's no one else. And since I'm going, since I have the responsibility for everyone on board this vessel, I must know that message.'

" 'You don't need to know it. They'll know on shore. All you have to do is to make contact.'

He wasn't prepared to take that. He dug his heels in.

" 'Understand this – if I'm not given that message, I don't leave this ship.'

" 'I see. An ultimatum.'

" 'If you like.'

" 'Then I don't have much choice,' I said, 'do I?'

" 'Not really.'

"So I gave him what he wanted. 'Very well. The coded message I expect to see is: *Vengeance is mine, says the Lord.*'

" '*Vengeance is mine, says the Lord,*' he repeated. 'Right. That's what you'll see. And that I promise you.'

Again the man at the desk looked up at me with his intent gaze, as he continued.

"And that's the message I did see. About 2.30 a.m., when we were lying about 8 kilometres from the coast. And a terrible dilemma it placed me in. Because it was the wrong message."

For the first time since he'd begun his story, I interrupted him.

"The wrong message? What do you mean? Wasn't that the message you'd asked to see – that you'd expected to see?"

"No, no, no!" he said. And he thumped the desk in front of him. "You see, I hadn't trusted Hans Utterman, not from the start. I didn't know if he was a genuine Palmach man, or a spy cleverly infiltrated by the British. I'd been forced to use him to get a message to shore, but I was damned if I'd let him have the current Haganah code. So what I gave him was the code used in the previous 17–day period – of course we changed them from time to time.

"It all seemed so simple. If Utterman was genuine and made contact with the reception committee, they'd know the current code and use it. If he was a fake, a spy, then he'd go straight to the British and tell them about us – a ship loaded to the gunwales with illegal immigrants only a kilometre or two from shore. They might even use the code to try and lure us further inshore.

"So if I saw the message I'd given him, the thing to do was to turn round as quickly as possible and head straight out for sea."

"Good God!" I said. "But it wasn't as simple as that, was it? Didn't you consider a third possibility?"

"Only after he'd gone. Only then it struck me. Only then I realised in what a dilemma I might have placed our friends on shore. You see, suppose this Utterman was genuine, and suppose he told the committee that I was expecting to see the message: *Vengeance is mine, says the Lord* – that he'd promised me faithfully that this would be the message I'd see. Would the committee flash me the code I said I was expecting? Or would they flash the one I ought to be expecting?"

"And the message you got...?" I asked.

"The wrong one," he said. "The wrong one. The one I'd given to Hans Utterman."

"So what did you do?"

The old man looked anguished.

"The wrong thing. To my eternal shame, the wrong thing. I put my trust, against my better judgment, in that damned German spy. I convinced myself that he'd argued with the reception committee, that he'd insisted they flash the message I'd told him I expected to see. That message, shining out from the top of Mount Carmel over the calm sea – wrong though it was, it seemed like a beacon of hope. Surely our own people were out there in the darkness, only a little way away, waiting for us. Transport, shelter, an end to the long, long pilgrimage. The haven awaited, the only haven for a Jewish heart.

"I gave the order to move forward the last few kilometres. We inched ahead in the darkness, closer and closer. Suddenly... lights, brilliant, brilliant lights, flooded the ship from stem to stern. And that voice, that British voice I hear still in my dreams, my nightmares . . .

" 'Stand to, the *Miriam*. You are surrounded. You will be boarded shortly. My men have orders to fire if there is any resistance. Keep calm and no–one will be hurt.'

"Motor vessels burst into life and roared towards us. Within minutes we were surrounded. We offered no resistance when they boarded us.

"We were all interned, every last one of us, first on shore, then in Cyprus, for over a year. For myself I didn't care. But those people, so close after so long, after so much tribulation – only to have the cup dashed from their lips. It was heart–breaking. As soon as I got back, I set myself the job of tracking down that German spy. I scoured the country. While I served my time in the Navy, I went on looking. I never saw or heard of him in all that time. Then I took this job in the Illegal Immigration Museum because I knew that, if he was still alive, then one day the museum would draw him. For the last twenty years I've sat here, searching the faces – always in vain. Until..."

"Until today," I said. "That's right isn't it, Uzzi? You recognised Hans Utterman the minute he walked through that door."

"Of course," said Uzzi Tal. "I didn't know if you recognised me, but as far as I'm concerned age, weight, an accent – what are they? The man is in the eyes. The eyes you can't disguise. At last."

His right hand moved to his desk drawer, and a second later a revolver was pointing directly at me.

"I'm sorry about your grandchildren, Herr Utterman. They're innocent. But the time has come to pay for your betrayal. As you see, I'm prepared. I've been prepared all these years."

I made no move of any sort.

"Put your gun away, Uzzi. Listen to what I have to say."

"You think you can talk your way out of this?" he said. "For forty years that betrayal has eaten away at my mind. For forty years I've waited to avenge that terrible wrong. And you think you can talk your way out of it?"

"I think you should face the truth," I said, "not go on chasing 40-year-old illusions."

His voice reflected the anguish in his mind.

"Illusions? Is that what you call one of the great betrayals of the Jewish struggle?"

"Illusions," I insisted. "You've got it all wrong. It never happened as you thought. Do you want to hear the truth? Can you bear it?"

Uzzi Tal slumped back in his chair, though the gun in his hand remained pointing straight at me.

"Tell me."

"That night," I said, "I got to shore about 1 a.m., beached the boat, shipped the oars, and walked across the sand – straight into the arms of a British patrol. I was captured almost at once."

"Whether you were a paid informer," said Tal, "or whether you cracked under a little interrogation – what does it matter?"

"I didn't crack," I said. "I didn't need to. I was taken to British headquarters, and it was quite clear that they knew the *Miriam* was out there. She'd been tracked halfway across the Mediterranean. They'd also broken the Haganah code – or so I'd believed until just this moment. Now I realise that all they had was the old code – they didn't know it had been changed.

"They decided to make things easy for themselves by flashing out to the ship what they thought was the reception message. The closer to shore the *Miriam* came, the more likely they could board her and intern the passengers without much trouble.

"You, my dear Uzzi, made two classical errors: you under-estimated the enemy, and you were too suspicious of your friends. The result was disaster – and you brought the disaster on yourself. If only you'd given me the right code in the first place, the whole tragedy would never have happened. You'd have received the wrong message, and you could have got away."

Tal lowered the revolver. In the dim greenish light, I could see that his hand was shaking.

"How have you turned up after 40 years? Why could I never find you?"

"I was shipped by the British straight back to my country of origin," I said, "to Germany. They did that, you know, whenever they could. I didn't manage to return to Israel till '49. I got married – yes, the same girl – and settled down in the Negev. I took a Hebrew name, and over the years I've lost my German accent. But Avraham Ramon or Hans Utterman, I'm the same man, quite innocent of the crimes you've been charging me with in your heart all these years. If there is any guilt for the extra misery heaped upon those hapless refugees – where does it lie? You tell me.

"Uzzi, you've been nurturing vengeance in this place for twenty years. Once it takes root, vengeance is a plant that thrives in the shadows. Pull back the blinds, let in the light, and it will shrivel and fade away. No, vengeance isn't for us mortals, Uzzi. Remember – "Vengeance is mine, says the Lord."

\*

The convoluted politics of the Muslim states surrounding Israel, and the shifting patterns of contacts and semi-alliances in which Israel engaged, left most observers more than a trifle confused. These relationships, in the period prior to the first Gulf war, assume more than an academic interest in the light of the results of the second. While the Iran-Iraq war was still in full flood, I tried to throw some light into a few dark corners, in an article published in the *Jewish Herald* on 10 December 1987.

# WHAT IS ISRAEL UP TO IN THE GULF?

*Jerusalem.*

What is Israel up to in the Gulf, and why? It's a conundrum as nagging an irritant as the pea beneath the princess's mattress.

If there is a consistent theme running through Gulf politics, it is the rabid hatred the Khomeini regime professes for all things Israeli, which it lumps together with all things Western in general and all things American in particular. Linked to the all-encompassing enmity for the Zionist state is the Ayatollah's oft–proclaimed objective to "liberate" Jerusalem. Yet it is to Iran that American and Israeli–made weapons have been consistently finding their way throughout the conflict, and the various arms–for-hostages deals have seen Israel acting as honest broker. Israel, until recently at least, seems to have adopted a clear pro–Iranian stance. What can explain a country persistently supporting its declared enemy?

When the Iran–Iraq conflict broke out in September 1980, existing tensions in the surrounding Arab states were consolidated. Most of the Arab world lined up in support of Iraq – the solid, centralist, Moslem state that had sent a fighting contingent to support the Arab cause in all the major conflicts with Israel. Syria, however, did not fall into line. Influenced, perhaps, by his long–standing personal hostility to Saddam Hussein, perhaps by the ancient split between the Ba'athist parties in the two countries, Syria's Assad, supported by Libya's Gaddafi, threw his weight behind Iran.

But the pro–Soviet, pro-Persian axis represented little threat to Israel. From Israel's point of view it was the pro-Iraqi line–up that was the key to the situation. Iraq represented the Arab enemy – six divisions of it – and was supported by the bulk of the Arab world including Jordan and Saudi Arabia. Iran's military machine was rudimentary compared to Iraq's, and was heavily dependent – as it has remained – on U.S. weaponry, originally purchased by the Shah. In fact, according to the speaker of Iran's Parliament, Ali Akbar Hashem Rafsanjani – probably the most powerful man in Iran after Khomeini – Iran has been obliged throughout the conflict to continue to buy American weapons on the open market.

Israeli military intelligence perceived a long–term interest in keeping open channels with Iran, especially those which foster the flow of military materials. The change of regime from Shah to Ayatollah cannot, it is argued, alter the geopolitical realities. In 1980, of course, the full–scale nature of the Islamic fundamentalist philosophy and its translation into unrestrained revolutionary action was not yet fully appreciated. And Iran did not, like Iraq, have a long history of open conflict with Israel.

More to the point, Khomeini would not live forever, and his regime was unlikely to persist unaltered after his death.

So the strategy was to hold off an Iraqi victory and keep the channels with Iran open in the hope of re–establishing effective working relationships with more moderate elements, if or when they emerged. Redressing the military balance in Iran's favour was a useful step in that direction.

However, Israel's policy, which made some sort of sense at the start of the conflict, seems to become progressively less relevant as Iran gains the upper hand. The old argument about keeping Israel's enemies occupied in fighting each other loses its point once an Iranian victory begins to seem possible.

Just imagine the implications if Iran, a radical anti-Western, Shi–ite, Moslem fundamentalist state were suddenly triumphant and dominant in the Middle East. Iran's victory would mean Islamist Militancy on the rampage. There would be no holding Libya, or Syria, or indeed the Shi–ite elements in Lebanon – a situation scarcely calculated to improve the prospects of peace on Israel's northern border.

Egypt, Jordan and Saudi Arabia, on the other hand, would be forced back on the defensive, at least in respect of their view of what Islam is all about. There is some evidence that Egypt, recognising the dangers in Israel's support of Iran, has pulled back from pursuing at least one initiative that might have opened the way to a limited pro–Western Arab alliance.

Meanwhile Israel's reported arms sales to Iran have not gone unchallenged inside Israel itself. Earlier in the year there was a degree of public unease at the thought that the interests of Israel's arms dealers might be dictating the country's foreign policy. All arms transactions are supposed to be reported to a Knesset subcommittee specifically charged with this topic.

Cash from arms deals with Iran certainly provides a useful addition to Israel's balance of payments, although how long the goose can go on laying golden eggs is open to speculation. In an interview for the Iranian daily newspaper, *Ettela'at,* Speaker Rafsanjani said that over the last year the conflict had cost Iran nearly £2 billion, and that the war effort was biting hard on the poor.

He claimed he was doubtful about the wisdom of asking people to endure yet more financial hardship – he said nothing of the continued wholesale slaughter of teenagers – in pursuit of a new all–out offensive against Iraq. How much of this was information and how much disinformation, though, is anyone's guess.

Nevertheless, all in all, it seems as though the changing fortunes of war are about to force Israel into a reappraisal of its long–standing strategy in the Gulf. Indeed, Foreign Minister Peres, in recent

speeches during his visit to Europe, has been at pains to stress that
arms sales to Iran are a thing of the past, and that Iraq is to be com-
mended for confronting its extreme fundamentalist neighbour.

*The Jewish Herald*
*10 December 1987*

\*

At roughly the same time, extraordinary developments
appeared to be taking, or to have taken, or to be about to take,
place in the on-going Israel-Palestinian struggle. Rumours of
a breakthrough in negotiations swept the country. Was there
anything in them? Were the parties claiming them subject to a
sort of mass delusion? Could the denials be believed? Who was
fooling who?

# WISHFUL THINKING?

*Jerusalem*

What exactly did Yasser Arafat say to Charlie Biton before the
lights went out in Geneva? That's what has been keeping half Israel
guessing, for the past week – especially since the immediate consequence, according to Biton, leader of a team of left–wing Knesset
members and others from Israel to the recent UN conference on the
Palestine question, was that the four MKs ended by hugging and
kissing Yasser Arafat.

The story in Israel since the four members of the Knesset flew
back from Geneva has centred on a "secret message" carried by
Charlie Biton from the PLO leader, and intended solely for the ears
of Prime Minister Yitzhak Shamir and Foreign Minister Shimon
Peres. According to Biton, the message is "radical, new and extreme."
It would need to be, for thee open statements of the PLO leader in

Geneva have remained jejune. He has simply reiterated that the PLO is ready to participate in a peace conference based on UN Security Council Resolutions 242 and 338, among others.

It is those "others" that are the problem.. Arafat's declaration is essentially the same as his proposal in February 1986, which King Hussein rejected as inadequate and which led to the failure of their talks. The Jordanian monarch realised then that to lump in a batch of UN General Assembly resolutions, like the one equating Zionism with racism, with the Security Council's 242 and 338, would be to scuttle any peace effort before it was even launched. It is not, therefore, surprising that Amman's reaction to the latest turn of events has been to express concern at the possibility of a "secret bilateral deal".

Who are Charlie Biton and his colleagues? The four MKs represent the left-wing Democratic Front for Peace and Equality in Israel's Parliament. Other members of the delegation included well-known peace activists like David Ish-Shalom ("Man of Peace") and Avi Oz. In dealing directly with the PLO they were sailing very close to the wind, and may yet find that some have capsized. The Attorney-General is deciding whether to initiate criminal proceedings. It is an offence under Israeli law to have dealings with terrorist organisations or those dedicated to the overthrow of the State. The PLO is regarded as meeting both criteria. However MKs who commit offences "in the course.of their duty" are granted immunity, and the four might well escape prosecution on those grounds. The fate of the other members of the delegation will probably turn on the outcome of current criminal proceedings being heard by the Ramle Magistrates Court against four left-wing peace activists who met PLO officials in Rumania last November.

Meanwhile Prime Minister Shamir and Foreign Minister Peres, while indicating no great enthusiasm for Charlie Biton's initiative, have both arranged for representatives to meet him and receive whatever message he has to deliver – this despite the fact, as Peres pointed out in a broadcast on Israel radio, that reports of secret Arafat proposals arrived in Israel virtually simultaneously with denials from within the PLO leadership that Arafat had made any such overture.

Can we at least get to the truth of this? Not really. Straight after Geneva, PLO spokesman Ahmed Abdul Rahman said in Tunis: "There is no message from Arafat relayed through the member of the Israeli parliament." Subsequently there have been denials from other PLO representatives, such as Abu–Mazen, of particular accounts of what Arafat may have said. According to Charlie Biton, though, "Who could deny it? All the top brass of the PLO were there, and I had two people with me at the meeting with Arafat."

As yet Biton has not formally revealed the contents of his message to the public, though versions are legion. Early speculation was to the effect that Arafat was calling simply for open and direct negotiations between Israel and the PLO, by–passing any international conference – hence Amman's startled reaction. To this, at least, Biton has given the lie. Later reports suggest that the offer is to negotiate with Israel through an international conference.

A more detailed account, emanating from Geneva, speaks of three PLO "bases" (not "conditions") for entering negotiations with Israel within the framework of an international conference: mutual cessation of hostilities, a freeze on settlement activity during the negotiations, and mutual recognition between Israel and the PLO.

Reaction in official circles to all this has been sceptical in the extreme. Most leading political figures regard the whole exercise as a public relations ploy by Arafat, by Biton or by both. Peres is still actively pursuing his aim of an international peace conference to be held under the aegis of the five permanent members of the Security Council, and is reportedly carrying Jordan's King Hussein along with him. For Peres to accept Arafat's overture – if it was really made – could not only jeopardise much that has already been achieved, but could provide the Likud with a stout political stick with which to beat the opposition.

Prime Minister Shamir, borne rather reluctantly along on the peace talks wave, takes his stand on the Camp David accords and favours an arrangement that would be limited to the parties most closely involved. Both scenarios certainly envisage direct Palestinian involvement; neither would countenance a place for the PLO as such at the negotiating table, short of a declaration which met the so–called "Yariv–Shemtov formula" (renunciation by the PLO of terrorism, and recognition of Israel and her right to exist) – and perhaps not even then, depending on who led from the Israeli side.

Hence, it is surmised, arises the PLO's Geneva initiative. If it actually occurred, it emanates from the conclusions of the 18th Palestine National Council (PNC) held in Algiers earlier this year. The strategy agreed at that PNC was to build on contacts with any democratic forces inside Israel that support the Palestinian interest. The 18th PNC saw a reuniting of mainstream and left–wing factions within the PLO, and although George Habash (of the PFLP) and Naif Hawatme (of the DFLP) opposed the resolution on Israeli contacts, they went along with it for the sake of new–found unity.

In fact, the latest position represents the development of a line agreed in resolutions passed at earlier PNC meetings. The 13th PNC, for example, defined permissible Israeli contacts only in terms of democratic Jewish officials opposed to Zionism in theory and practice. By the 16th PNC this had been broadened somewhat to embrace Israelis who support Palestinian self–determination. The new 18th PNC definition, for the first time includes Israeli Zionists among those whom PLO officials may meet. Matti Steinberg, an expert on the PLO working at the Hebrew University in Jerusalem, ascribes this extension of permissible Israeli contacts mainly to Yasser Arafat who, he says, has pushed for this policy against the opposition of other factions within the PLO.

Arafat and others of his way of thinking see a double benefit from the policy: a way of extending PLO influence inside Israel, and a device to help polarise already strongly–held views within Israeli society on solving the Palestine problem.

Opposing Arafat's approach are the reunited left–wing factions: the PFLP, the DFLP and the Palestine Communist Party. They see the PLO's main hope of achieving its objectives as an international conference at which they would rely on the support of the USSR.

Also opposed to the Arafat line is a group of influential main–line Fatah figures, though for different reasons. They see any increase in PLO contacts with Israel as an overt sign of approval of growing Israeli–Arab contacts elsewhere (Egypt, Jordan, Morocco), all of which tend to by–pass the PLO. This group sees nothing for the PLO in an international conference, and is calling instead for an intensification of the armed struggle. Sabri Jiris, editor of the PLO's magazine "Shu'un Filistiniya" represented these views in a recent outspoken article which strongly attacked the PLO leadership for lack of steadfastness.

With such a line–up of vested interests in both Israeli and Palestinian camps, what hope is there for any Arafat–Biton initiative, always supposing it is no chimera? Arafat may just have thought it worthwhile to wink in Biton's direction at Geneva, in line with agreed PNC strategy. It is certain that Biton – despite his threat, if he is not taken seriously, to publish and be damned – is likely to continue to get very short shrift from the Prime Minister's Office and, for rather different reasons, from the Foreign Minister's. Wishful thinkers inside Israel, though, are already having a field day. One of the objects, perhaps, of the exercise?

\*

A rarely considered aspect of Israel's foreign policy suddenly surfaced in the middle of this 40<sup>th</sup> anniversary year – her relations with Black Africa. A little research revealed a fascinating and consistent strategy on Israel's part – complicated, somewhat, by her historic ties with what was still then White South Africa (ties wholly understandable, in the light of South Africa's large Jewish population). In May 1988, I attempted to unravel the story).

# ISRAEL IN BLACK AFRICA

The news this week that Israel is forging ties with the black opposition in South Africa marks a new development in an old story.

A formal invitation has gone out to the black communities in South Africa to send representatives on courses to be held in Jerusalem and elsewhere in Israel – a small and apparently innocuous step. In fact the move marks a major change of direction in Israel's relations with South Africa, and its importance is evidenced by the furious reaction of the South African government.

The move follows pressures from various sources – the US Congress, the United Nations – to cut the full–scale links with South Africa, and especially arms sales, hitherto maintained by Israel. The step was not taken without a deal of heart–searching. White South Africa has proved a consistent and loyal friend to Israel. But the inevitable logic of the African situation has at last, inevitably, come to dictate Israel's political stance. It is clear that in the long run (perhaps even the medium run) the black communities in South Africa will come to have a dominant political role in running the country. Israel cannot afford to be at odds with them.

In fact, there is nothing surprising in this move on Israel's part. It fits absolutely logically into a strategy with deep roots in Israel's foreign policy.

It was after Israel's brilliantly daring coup at Entebbe airport on 4 July 1976, when a plane–load of hostages was snatched from under President Idi Amin's nose, that the wider public first learned of the scale of Israel's network of connections in black Africa. The operation, it was apparent, had been possible only because Israel possessed detailed plans of Uganda's airport building (not surprising since an Israeli construction company had designed and built part of it), and because President Kenyatta had been content to authorise both an overflight by the Israeli rescue planes across Kenya's airspace, and a refuelling stop at Nairobi airport. Indeed the *Jerusalem Post*, on the morning after the raid, reported that several of the rescued passengers were being treated in a Nairobi hospital.

Entebbe represented a hugely satisfactory pay–off for years of patient investment by Israel in black Africa. A basic principle underlying Israel's foreign policy during the state's early years had, of necessity, been to cultivate friends wherever she could find them. Accordingly, during the 1950s and 1960s, despite sometimes stringent economic difficulties at home, Israel consistently provided military and technical expertise in a variety of specialised fields to any African state prepared to establish friendly relations with her,

The Jewish connection with the North African mediterranean belt goes back to biblical times, and even today, though relationships are wary, it is Egypt and Morocco alone among the Arab states that are prepared to deal with Israeli leaders openly.

The connection with black Africa goes back almost as far. One of the early waves of Jewish dispersion flowed through Ethiopia, and the title "Lion of Judah" somehow became attached to the Emperor. His mixed bag of peoples were claimed by some to be the Ten Lost Tribes. One section at least, the Falashas, retained sufficient of their Jewish identity to make good their claim to be an integral element of the Jewish people. Now, of course, as they are permitted to leave Ethiopia, they are being absorbed into the body proper of Israel.

The strategic reality that Israel learned to live with, from her earliest days, was that she was ringed with hostile Arab neighbours, all more or less intent on her destruction. A prime foreign policy objective that quickly emerged, therefore, was to construct as complete an outer circle of friendly states as possible. Black Africa represented a key element in the encirclement strategy.

The Uganda connection went back to the 1950s. Israeli diplomats stationed in Kenya during Mau Mau days were in touch with Dr Milton Obote well before he became Uganda's first president. Immediately afterwards, Israel was invited to help establish and train the new Ugandan army and air force. Under the terms of a 1963 agreement she despatched a military mission to Kampala to begin the process.

Through an open–handed policy of financial, technical and military aid over the 1960s and early 1970s, Israel succeeded in establishing a working relationship with an impressive cross-section of black Africa – impressive since a number are basically Islamic, but also since at no time did Israel disrupt her traditionally close ties with South Africa. These essentially patron–client relationships, in which the deal was technology in exchange for recognition, were always somewhat strained – if only because the patron was always in some respects as vulnerable economically and politically as its clients.

The Arab–Israel war of 1973 upset what seemed to have become a settled pattern. With the exception of Swaziland, Lesotho and Malawi, all Israel's "client states" broke off relations. Moral outrage was insignificant as a factor compared with the combination of threats and promises from the Arab states – threats of unspecified financial action and promises of untold quantities of financial aid. In the event neither materialised, and disillusionment with the Arab world has long since set in, no doubt fostered by apprehension at Colonel Gaddafi's unpredictable ambitions in the continent in general, and Chad in particular.

In spite of – perhaps because of – an absence of normal diplomatic relations, Israel has succeeded over the past decade in rebuilding an African connection. One by one the Ivory Coast, Cameroon, Liberia and Zaire have restored relations; Kenya, Ghana and Gabon now permit Israel to run missions inside their countries. Last July the Israeli Prime Minister, Yitzhak Shamir, completed a tour of selected West African states to cement relations. As a result Togo became the fifth black African country to restore formal ties with Israel.

The Government's policy, which seems so logical in theory, did not go unchallenged inside Israel. In particular, some voices questioned its discriminating nature. Friends at any price" may have been both expedient and generally acceptable in the '50S and '60s; it did not seem to suit everybody in the moral '80s. An Israel that could equivocate over its ties with South Africa, despite the vastly important Jewish community it contains, can scarcely climb into bed with the likes of Presidents Samuel Doe of Liberia or Paul Biya of Cameroon, without a squeak of protest from one quarter or another.

The latest evidence of a positive attitude towards the black opposition within South Africa, and the weakening of Israel's South African connection, will serve to restore a degree of bipartisanship to an issue that was threatening to become a cause of major political contention within Israel. Meanwhile, the first party of black South Africans are already in Israel, and more are awaited.

*

In the dying days of 1987 I travelled to Japan. I was not in the country very long before two inescapable facts forced themselves on my attention – the Jewish community was tiny, and the anti-Semitism was huge. I sought out the Jewish centre in Tokyo, which incorporated the only synagogue, and I talked to the rabbi and to other Jewish contacts. When I got home, I wrote a piece for the *Jewish Chronicle*, which was published in the issue of 12 August 1988.

# LAND OF THE RISING HATE

The taxi–driver at Ebisui station, in one of Tokyo's south–western suburbs, had never heard of the Jewish Community Centre. He puzzled long and earnestly over the Japanese script in which a helpful hotel clerk had inscribed the address.

At length, with a shrug, he set off. Turning a corner, he drove up a short, steep street, apparently without much hope, and seemed astonished when a cry from the rear seat told him to stop.

If we had been able to speak fluently to one another, he would doubtless have asked: "How on earth did you know which building it was?" To which the reply – in the form of a question, naturally, coming from a Jew – might have been: "How could you not know the Jewish Community Centre when its facade is embellished with a Magen David that must rank as one of the largest on public display anywhere!"

And yet, in one way, the incident is not surprising. Metaphorically, you can almost count the Jewish community in Japan on the fingers of one hand. More prosaically, if you started counting, you would not be able to reach 1,000.

There is, in fact, virtually no indigenous Jewish population. The thousand individuals are mainly youngish temporary immigrants working for the large international corporations, together with a small floating contingent of Israeli families attached to the embassy – perhaps two dozen in all.

There are only about half–a–dozen well-established Jewish families: they landed up in Japan as a result of immigration from Russia via China during the past century – centred on Tokyo and on the port city of Kobe, about 300 miles away.

How surprising, then, to find in a Tokyo suburb a spacious modern building, comfortingly well–protected by the latest electronic devices. A press of the Telescan button, a long wait outside the heavy metal doors and, one presumed, a searching scrutiny through the TV camera, eventually resulted in the click of the lock.

Unexpected as the building is on the outside, the interior is, quite frankly, astonishing. A large public area on the ground floor, one wall covered by a notice–board revealing a wide variety of communal activities, leads up to a large, comfortably furnished first–floor library, flanked on one side by a well–upholstered sitting area and a television room, the whole opening out on to a covered terrace and a full-length outdoor swimming pool.

Climb the wide staircase to the second floor, and there, to your amazement, is a spacious, beautifully appointed synagogue with, to one side, cheder classrooms, a rabbi's office and a specialised Judaica library.

"And in the basement," announces the Israeli–born caretaker–cum–guard, "we have a fully equipped mikva, complete with showers."

The notice–board outside the synagogue proclaims that services are held regularly on Friday night and Shabbat and that kosher meals are available. It also reveals that the minister in attendance is Rabbi Michael J. Schudrich.

"I arrived here from New York in 1983," 32-year–old Rabbi Schudrich told me. "The community decided to look to the Conservative movement for a rabbi and, having gained my semicha through the Jewish Theological Seminary in New York, I qualified.

The challenge interested me and, together, my wife and I decided that I should apply. We came over to Japan for a trial period, and I was offered the job."

Rabbi Schudrich said that, although there had always been a few scattered Jewish families in Japan – some lived in Nagasaki at the end of the last century, and a few settled later in Yokahama and Kobe – the Second World War saw no increase at all in Jewish settlement, and in 1948 there were probably no more than six Jewish families in the whole of Japan.

Three years later, there had been enough of an inflow to warrant the establishment of a Jewish community on a formal basis. Under its first president, Anatole Pouve, the board of management, representing Jewish life in Tokyo, decided to purchase a house and a large plot of land in a pleasant suburb of the city, and there, in 1953, the original community centre opened its doors.

Five years later, the decision was taken to rationalise the original land purchase in order to fund the design and construction of a modern building, with a range of facilities. The idea was that such a centre could become a real focus for the lives of those Jews whom circumstances drew to Japan, either temporarily or on a permanent basis.

Accordingly, some 60 per cent of the land was sold for development, and an architect was engaged to design the building which now serves the Tokyo community. In doing so, he managed to preserve part of the original construction, which has genuine historical value. The proceeds of the land sale served not only to pay for the new building, but, with the remainder invested, to help maintain it.

The centre owes its impressive synagogue to one of the great names of the Japanese Jewish story – Shaul Nehemiah Halevi Eisenberg, president from 1964 to 1969. Eisenberg, now elderly and out of the country, has his abiding memorial in the Beth David Synagogue, whose plaque records its dedication on November 7, 1968, in honour of his parents.

Today, the president of the board is Walter J. Citrin. As a representative of the very few long-term residents, he is well–qualified. He took over the presidency from Eisenberg in 1969 and initially served for twelve years. Last year, he assumed office for a second time.

The Beth David Synagogue conducts its services Ashkenazi style; there is, in fact, another shul serving the small community in Kobe – although without a rabbi – which conforms to the Sephardi tradition. The representative Jewish voices of Japan therefore constitute a triumvirate: Rabbi Schudrich; the president of the Tokyo community, Walter Citrin; and the Israeli Ambassador, the popular Yaakov Cohen.

Asking Rabbi Schudrich about the challenges now facing the Jewish community in Japan, I fully expected him to detail the extraordinary upsurge of antisemitic literature currently achieving monumental sales among middle– and upper–class Japanese (over 600,000 copies of one particular farrago of virulent nonsense were sold last year); or perhaps the tenacious adherence to the Arab boycott by most Japanese industrial and commercial organisations; or perhaps even the studied exclusion of Jerusalem's Mayor, Teddy Kollek, from the invitations sent to the mayors of the world's historic cities to mark the 1,200th anniversary of the founding of Kyoto (and which city in the world is more historic than Jerusalem?).

But no. Rabbi Schudrich believed that, while each of these phenomena was in itself annoying and regrettable, and demonstrated the long road still to travel in the effort to bring Japan and Israel (in the widest sense) closer together, they did not constitute a sinister pattern.

"It is absurd to suggest that the Japanese are antisemitic in the Nazi sense or, indeed, in any sense familiar to Europeans. The Japanese have no experience of Jews on which to base any such views. What we are seeing is a sort of trendy conspiracy theory feeding on current apprehensions in the financial and business worlds."

The 80–odd venomously antisemitic books currently on sale in Japan all have the word "Jew" in the title in order to cash in on the market, and Rabbi Schudrich is sure that the authors like the xenophobic Masami Uno, parliamentarian Aisaburo Saito, and leading entrepreneur Den Fujita, holder of the McDonald's franchise in Japan – are simply jumping on a lucrative bandwagon without any real understanding of what they are doing, or how the rest of the world will view their activities.

The commercial tide is running so strongly that one publisher is happily making a fast buck out of a new edition of the Japanese translation of the notorious forgery, "The Protocols of the Elders of Zion," used extensively by Nazi propagandists. It was originally translated into Japanese in the early 1920s and enjoyed a great vogue during the Nazi era.

One member of Tokyo's Jewish community, temporary English expatriate Jonathan Isaacs, was sufficiently alarmed by all this, and by the appearance of nationalist posters featuring the swastika, to write to the Jewish Chronicle last summer, and he repeated his misgivings at greater length in the Wall Street Journal.

"Frankly, I'm extremely worried," Isaacs told me. "The anti–Jewish situation here, absurd though it is with so few Jews, bears all the hallmarks of the rise of antisemitism in pre–war Europe. We have to learn the lessons of the past, stand up and be counted. We must not allow ignorant and wicked calumnies against the Jewish people to go unchallenged. We must oppose the Arab boycott wherever it is practised."

Now at least one or two Japanese voices are being raised against the current antisemitic wave. Literary critic Takeshi Muramatsu, in a well–argued article reprinted in an English language newspaper, has called it "the unacceptable face of popular Japanese journalism."

Author Masahiro Miyazaki has also come forward to oppose the current fad. In a new book, he offers Japanese readers a rational explanation of the financial and business problems facing the country, refuting the idea that there could be any reasons for Japan becoming a breeding ground for a new growth of virulent antisemitism.

Rabbi Schudrich goes along with Miyazaki's view and approach, believing that the fire, without substantial fuel to feed it, will burn itself out. He points particularly to recent signs that ties between Japan and Israel are beginning to strengthen, after years of stagnation. An article in the Asian edition of the Wall Street Journal points to a rapid rise in trade over the past few years between the two countries. This may have been undertaken, the paper believes, partly in an effort to improve US–Japanese relations – although always with a weather eye open on not disturbing Japan's huge favourable balance of trade with the Arab world – but that is not important in view of the end result.

"If we really wanted to boycott to please the Arabs," one Japanese trade official is reported as saying recently, "there would be absolutely no trade with Israel."

In fact, only last month the Japanese Foreign Minister, Mr Sosuke Uno, paid an official visit to Israel during which the question of trade and investment was often mentioned.

So Rabbi Schudrich sees good and bad in the current political scene, but no immediate or impending crisis for the Jewish interest.

"If you want to know what I really do regard as the major challenge facing all Japanese Jewry," he says, "it is how to solve the problem of building a rock–solid Jewish community life on the shifting sands of a largely temporary and fluctuating population. There really is no sense of permanence among those who make up my congregations."

*The Jewish Chronicle*
*12 August 1988*

*

While in Tokyo, an impish spirit moved me to write a letter to the editor of the only daily newspaper published in English in the capital, the *Mainichi Daily News*. It was printed in the issue of 28 November 1987.

The Editor,
The Mainichi Daily News.

Sir,

Visiting Tokyo briefly from the United Kingdom, it was pleasant – if a trifle surprising – to see that you had opened your columns to His Excellency the Ambassador of Jordan on the occasion of King Hussein's birthday. May we expect that, in the spirit of your admirable slogan "Dedicated to International Understanding", you will be inviting the ambassador of Israel to address your readers shortly on the 40th anniversary of the founding of the state of Israel? If not, I wonder whether, in the furtherance of the ideal of international understanding, you would be able to locate at least six Japanese firms willing to associate themselves with an advertisement of congratulations?

Yours etc.

\*

# THE PASSING SCENE – 3

With the extensive re–paving of Ben–Yehuda in central Jerusalem now complete, the street is virtually a pedestrian precinct. Except, of course, since this is Israel, for the occasional vehicle which seems permitted to ease its way past the shoppers and the proliferating café tables.

Sitting at one such the other day, sipping a *mitz eshcoliot* (grapefruit juice), I met up with a couple of brothers on leave from the forces. Gaby is starting the third of his three years in the army while Zev has just completed his pilot's training in the air force.

Gaby explained how, over his three years of military service, a young man slowly matures from raw recruit to experienced soldier. Promotion is pretty-well guaranteed as you progress, and Gaby, now a sergeant, is enjoying the prospect of bringing on a bunch of young recruits. In fact, he is enjoying it all so much that he is seriously thinking of applying for a commission and signing on for an extra year's service.

Zev explained the fearsomely tough selection procedure imposed by the Israeli air force in training its pilots. Less than 10 per cent of those who start the training get through to the high–spot recently enjoyed by Zev and his comrades–the passing–out parade. Zev himself explained how he came within a hair's breadth of rejection at one moment for being caught "improperly dressed". Now a fully–fledged pilot, he expects to enter the civil aviation field, once his military service is behind him.

*

Talking of matters military, I was walking through Tel Aviv when I happened to notice I was passing Rehov Ha'arbaa. This street name (the Street of the Four) is always associated in my mind with the Association for the Welfare of Israel's Soldiers, whose offices are at No 8. I decided to give my donation this year in person, and made my way up to the second floor.

And what a welcome I received!

Jews all over the world subscribe to this most worthy of charities, which concerns itself exclusively with the needs of soldiers in Israel. And that means caring for virtually all young people during their time in the forces, as well as for the regular soldiers.

The Association opens and operates clubs at army bases, provides entertainment and sports facilities for troops on active duty, sends gift parcels especially to new recruits on the Holy Days, takes care of soldiers with no family in Israel, builds and operates educational facilities for young people in uniform – to name a few eminently–worthy activities.

Donations flow into the Association from all over the world – it's one way for Jews to show their togetherness with the men and women whose job it is to defend Israel's borders. At the Association's HQ, each part of the world has its own section. Miriam, who heads the English section, greeted me with open arms – a donor in person is a rarity indeed.

Anyone looking for an entirely worthy charity in Israel to subscribe to direct, cutting out all middlemen, should give the Association serious consideration. One thing's for certain – you'll always be sure of a warm welcome at 8 Ha'arbaa Street!

*

Talking of worthy causes, I have just been escorted on a visit to the Central Archives of the Jewish People, a little known but fascinating repository of written records from all over the world and going back to the Middle Ages.

Housed in part of a building on the Hebrew University's Givat Ram campus, the arehives are supported by a small grant–in–aid from the Government. But as the Director, Aryeh Segall, explained, they are heavily dependent on private donations.

In the basement of the Sprinzak building, what look like vast metal filing cabinets slide back on rollers built into floor and ceiling to reveal case after case of priceless original documents which record the life of Jewish communities from every country.

"A couple of years ago," explained senior archivist Renato Spiegel, "there was a plan to rehouse the entire collection. As well as providing better storage facilities, we would have been able to mount exhibitions to let people see something of the treasures that have to remain hidden. Unfortunately the plan fell through for lack of funds – and since then the collection has continued to grow.

"This is part of the heritage of the Jewish people," added assistant archivist Adam Teller. "We need a generous benefactor."

It was certainly fascinating to be holding original documents signed by Disraeli's father and by Moses Montefiore. Others, ranging from Poland to Rangoon, and the 16th century to 1965, are there to be used by a few fortunate scholars, but the doors of this rich treasure house are virtually waiting to be opened up.

*

Wandering through the centre of Tel Aviv, I wondered why every other street corner had all its paving stones up, sand everywhere and two or three workmen beavering away. A friend with a friend in high places enlightened me. Tel Aviv's popular mayor, Shlomo Lahat ("Chich" to his friends) has instituted a street refurbishment programme that is going to result in beautiful broad red brick sidewalks at every major intersection in the city. And indeed, the pavements that have been completed, taken together with the impressive new seafront promenade, add up to a vast improvement in the general look of the city. All part of long–term plans to build up Tel Aviv into one of the world's leading tourist attractions, I gather.

*

Bethlehem is looking noticeably more prosperous these days. Flourishing villas have spread into the hinterland that borders the main road to Hebron, and the number of new factories and houses that are going up as one drives through are impressive.

The old refugee camp at Da–Haisha, just outside the town, is still there, but it seems increasingly anomalous in what is obviously a thriving Arab community.

Of course tourism will always be a vital factor in Bethlehem's economy, but the town now seems to be spreading its wings into new commercial, industrial and agricultural enterprises.

Recent statistical reports speak of economic growth rates of 9 per cent a year in the West Bank over the past two years – and it shows.

\*

You know you're in Israel when, standing in the middle of a long queue at the checkout of your local supermarket, you get into conversation with a former Prisoner of Zion who escaped, back in 1970, from a Soviet prison camp and made his own perilous way to Israel.

In an appealing mixture of Hebrew, Russian, Yiddish and English, the ex–prisoner (1 shan't give his name) beguiled the long wait – which, I may say, is usually just as tedious in Israel as in the local Tesco.

Although human beings the world over are an inexhaustible source of fascination, I doubt if anywhere on earth boasts such a concentration of individuals with intensely dramatic backgrounds and personal histories as Israel. Any apparently ordinary middle–aged man or woman you encounter is quite likely to have a tale to tell that would make an action-packed movie in its own right.

For example, I made friends with a professional Israeli and his wife some years ago. It was a long time before I learnt that, as a little boy of six in Europe, he'd been sent to a series of concentration camps with his mother and, after a succession of hair–raising adventures, had been one of the few to be repatriated to Palestine from Germany at the end of the War. Their story, which his mother wrote as a book called *"Hand in Hand With Tommy,* has been selling steadily.

*

When the *Jerusalem Post* can legitimately publish a Good Food Guide, you know something has happened to eating out in Jerusalem. It may be going a little far to categorise the change as a revolution, but things are certainly looking up. New restaurants abound, many now also offering takeaway or a meals delivery service. Among such is the new *Mata'amim Deli* in Ramot, specialising in good old–fashioned Yiddisher food, *Taster's Choice*, which takes telephone orders for a Shabbat or holiday meal and delivers it to the door, *La Pasta*, a brand–new Italian restaurant and takeaway, and the *Tai–Ki House* (its name, when you think about it, tells all) which combines an impressive range of Chinese cooking, all glatt kosher, and take–away.

In fact, Chinese restaurants are clearly a mushroom growth area, if one may put it so. Three new ones have just opened their doors: *Ten Li Chow*, spreading its wings from Tel Aviv and Ra'anana where branches have already established a reputation; *Charlie Chan*, in Lunz Street, which also advertises a take–away and fast delivery service; and, surprisingly, in Bethlehem's Manger Street, *Candy Chen*.

Some well–established Jerusalem restaurants have caught the mood of the moment and are re–decorating and expanding their premises or offering new attractions or more imaginative menus. Among these are the *Rondo* in King George Street, *Off The Square* (Zion Square, that is), and *Home Plus* off Heleni Ha–Malcha, which now provides live jazz performances every morning from 9.30 to noon.

The hotels are in on the act, too. The Ramada Renaissance now offers the public a choice of four restaurants, and the Hilton no less than five.

Fast foods in a variety of forms are also proliferating. A brand–new cheese–cake shop has just opened its doors in Yoel Solomon Street advertising over 20 "absolutely heavenly" flavours. And Burger Tivall offers – believe it or not – glatt kosher cheeseburgers. How? By using a soya meat–substitute. Lovers of traditional hamburgers and

Kentucky fried chicken are now catered for in two new branches of Burger Ranch – both strictly kosher.

The very latest craze of all, though, is the "baguette" – lengths of super–fresh French bread sliced lengthways and stuffed with mouth–watering fillings. Leading the field is *La Javanaise Speed Baguette*, which has just opened three new suburban outlets. The secret of success lies in the combination of oven-fresh bread (they advertise that fresh bread emerges from their ovens every 20 minutes) and the fillings – delicious concoctions like garlic cream cheese, Greek feta and cucumber, or a tart Bulgarian spread. Oh, and they deliver as well!

All this is not to say that the traditional eat–in–the-street favourites that spell Jerusalem to the seasoned tourist – pitta stuffed with falafel and salad, or the shwarma sliced fresh from the revolving spit – are not still very much in evidence. They are. It's a wonder how so comparatively small a population can consume so much food.

*

I decided to take yet another visit to the Holyland Hotel in Jerusalem to view the extraordinary model reproduction of the city of Jerusalem at the time of the Second Temple.

Almost every visitor to Jerusalem makes a trek to the Western Wall, and many go up to the Temple Mount which stretches above it. Most people get a quite false impression of these ancient sites – and, more importantly, of their relationship to each other.

Of course, today the Temple Mount is dominated by two great mosques – the Al Aqsa and the Dome of the Rock, the one plated in gold and the other in silver. But in Biblical times, as the remarkable model of ancient Jerusalem makes plain, the Temple Mount was indeed the site of the Temple.

As you wander round the model reconstruction of the old city of Jerusalem, you are able at regular intervals to pick up headphones and listen to a commentary in one of four languages that describes the particular area of the ancient city spread out before you.

The front of Herod's Temple is a magnificent piece of work. A vast white marble façade rises high into the air, topped by a row of gilded ornaments and decorated with a pair of terracotta columns which stand out in stark contrast. Beneath, great curved stone stairs lead into the Holy of Holies, flanked on either side by cloisters created by rows of stone columns. Before all this stretches a great paved area.

All this has, of course, completely vanished, so there is a real fascination in comparing the Western Wall in Herod's time with what remains of it today. It becomes apparent that it is now only about half as high as originally, and that it once genuinely enclosed the whole of the Temple area to a height of some 10 feet or more.

Make a trek to the model of ancient Jerusalem next time you are in Israel – it's not half as well known as it should be.

\*

And then, in July 1988, Iran suddenly sued for peace and the Iran-Iraq war was over. I tried to make sense of what had happened, from Israel's point of view. How strange some of these predictions appear, in the light of the subsequent and totally unforeseeable Gulf wars and their aftermath.

# WHAT PRICE PEACE?

*Jerusalem*

Even in the cacophony of sounds that is Middle East politics, an unexpected note can produce strange music. The news that Ayatollah Khomeini was sipping his poisoned chalice sent Israel into a rare spin. Iran suing for peace in 1988 had an impact roughly comparable to Egypt making its pre-emptive strike across the Suez Canal in 1973.

At first, like children in a tantrum, everyone looked for a scapegoat. They lighted on Israel's military intelligence services. By an unhappy coincidence, at the very moment the Iranians were announcing their unconditional acceptance of a ceasefire, an Israeli Defense Force intelligence officer was briefing the Knesset's Foreign Affairs and Defense Committee on the unlikelihood of an early end to the conflict. Members emerged from the committee room to a patent demonstration that the country's intelligence community had been caught napping. The committee re–convened to grill senior officers about the failure. Harsh words spilled over into the media. The ashes of past intelligence errors, both of omission and of commission, were raked over. Some political analysts tried to point out the impossibility of predicting the unpredictable, but the military intelligence services had been undeniably humiliated.

Their confidence badly shaken by the intelligence failure, politicians began voicing dark fears about the possible implications. To some it seemed obvious that if two of Israel's sworn enemies were suddenly released from knocking the hell out of each other, one or both was quite likely to turn its attention to knocking the hell out of Israel. Nor were they particularly sanguine about the possible outcome. The gloom and doom are best understood in the context of certain recent events.

Quite apart from the *intifada,* things have not been going Israel's way of late. Only a few weeks before Iran's peace move, Israeli public opinion had suddenly woken up to the build–up of missile strength in the Arab world. Sparked by China's sale of CSS–2 missiles to Saudi Arabia, concern was fuelled by the revelation that Brazil, Argentina and North Korea, to say nothing of the Soviet Union, were also supplying advanced ballistic weaponry to a host of Arab countries.

Syria, for example, had taken shipment of a further order of SS–21 battlefield support missiles from the USSR to top up their Frog–7s and Scud–Bs. The Scud–B, it was revealed, flying at three times the speed of sound and carrying a 500–kilogram warhead, could hit Tel

Aviv from a Damascus launch in five minutes. In addition, Syria was reported to be in contact with China about developing the new and more powerful M–9 missile.

Already in possession of Scud–Bs, Egypt was revealed to be collaborating with North Korea on a development project to manufacture her own, and with Argentina to develop the Condor3, an 800–kilometre range missile. Libya, too, has Scud–Bs, and was reported to be working with Brazil on a new line of missiles. No sooner had Israel begun digesting all this, than the news broke of Britain's massive arms deal with Saudi Arabia. No wonder that announcement assumed a disproportionate significance in the public mind at the time (though maturer consideration has since produced a more balanced view).

As for Iraq, it was well known that she had built up an impressive war machine over the eight years of the Gulf conflict. She had over a million men under arms, a tank force 5,000 strong, nearly 600 military aircraft and 36 surface–to–surface missiles. Iraq's Scud–B, known as the al–Husayn, had the range to hit Tel Aviv if fired from western Iraq, but she had also tested a longer–range version called the al–Abbas. It would take only 10%–15% of this largest and most experienced Arab military force to be redeployed in some anti–Israel alliance, as in 1973, completely to overturn the precarious balance of Arab/Israeli power. Added to the worry was the knowledge that the use of chemical weaponry had become almost standard battlefield procedure.

Iran's military strength, though much depleted, was also formidable. Was any of this likely to be deployed in any flare–up of the Arab–Israeli armed struggle?

Significantly, although both combatants had declared themselves implacable foes, neither had shirked a working relationship with Israel. Israel's sympathies had been engaged first on one side in the conflict, and then on the other. The Arab world had mostly regarded the fight as a war of Arab Iraq against non-Arab Iran – a view sustained by Israel's clear favouring of Iran when the conflict started.

In none of the Arab–Israeli wars had the Shah allied himself militarily with the Arab cause; Iraq, on the other hand, had sent fighting forces. In the early 1980s Israeli strategists tended to view the Ayatollah and his revolution as a passing phase. Khomeini is an old man, the argument went. Once he is gone, the geopolitical realities will reassert themselves. Meanwhile let us ensure that Iraq does not gain the upper hand.

These were the considerations that underlay Israel's destruction of Iraq's nuclear reactor and her sale of arms to Iran in defiance of the USA. The uneasy relationship thus established provided the context in which the 1986 US arms–for–hostages deal, Israel acting as "honest broker", very nearly came off.

More recently, with Syria gaining effective control of large areas of Lebanon, Iraq has found it necessary to reassess her position vis–a–vis Israel. It is a fact of political life that Syria's President Hafez Assad and Iraq's President Sadam Hussein hate each other's guts. Their relationship reflects the conflict between the rival Baathist parties of the Arab world that each represents. As Syria and Iran began forging an alliance of sorts and to set up a fundamentalist Shi'ite underground in Lebanon, Iraq drew closer to her more American-orientated neighbours. In any case, US aid was becoming increasingly vital to her.

The result, it now emerges, was a series of little publicised, but highly significant, overtures to Israel, largely rejected or turned aside by the Likud Government. Political analysts in Israel, following a lead given by Defense Minister Yitzhak Rabin – no political friend of the Prime Minister, and with an eye to the election campaign that is already in full swing – are regretting the "lost opportunities". Now it is being recalled that Iraq has promised no military aid to the intifada, nor indeed to any Arab state. Though her spokesmen still sometimes refer to the need to liberate Palestine, her only positive commitment in terms of the broader Arab/Israeli conflict has been a promise to come to Jordan's aid if attacked. Iraq, it is held, no longer regards herself as part of the rejectionist front and has made it known that she would not object to Israel's neighbours negotiating peace with Israel.

In any event, Iraq must be regarded by Syria as an extremely dubious ally in any future conflict with Israel. In the first place, it is far from certain that Iraq would hasten to the aid of the country that stabbed her in the back during her fight for survival against Iran. Far more likely she would welcome a Syrian defeat at Israel's hands as a just punishment. Nor would Syria necessarily regard a large-scale incursion of Iraqi armed forces on Israel's eastern front as an unmixed blessing. Against Iraq's 54 divisions, Syria can muster no more than 10. The possibility would always exist of being overwhelmed by Iraq's superior military strength should any alliance, which would in the nature of things be extremely uneasy, turn sour.

Whenever an Iran/Iraq peace treaty comes into effect, at least two factors will militate against any sudden upset of the balance of power. One is that continued suspicion will surely mark relations between the former combatants for a long time. The fighting that has served as an obligato to Perez de Cuellar's peace efforts is proof of that. The conflict has been too bitter and prolonged for any early or easy kissing and making up; mutual hostility will continue to absorb resources on both sides.

Then, one must take into account sheer battle fatigue and the economic and social devastation left in the wake of this most bloody of wars. Iran's teenage generation has been decimated; Iraq has lost almost one per cent of her population, and another two per cent are casualties. The war has caused both parties enormous economic losses. Neither is seeking further military enterprises to indulge in; rebuilding their shattered economies must be their first priority.

Attention is already swinging back to the main Arab/Israeli arena – the occupied territories. Within Israel, powerful political groups, looking to the November general election and beyond, are urging a more positive stance towards those of Israel's neighbours willing to deal.

King Hussein seems to be ceding his grandfather's dream of a Greater Jordan to the Palestinian's dream of an independent state, though self–interest probably features as much as disinterest in his recent disengagement from the West Bank. His move, no less that Iran's acceptance of UN Resolution 598, may have unpredictable consequences. Should the situation degenerate into armed conflict, though, it does not seem likely on present calculations that the Gulf War combatants would play a determining role.

\*

A few months later I was back in Israel, and I discerned a change in the political atmosphere – the early recognition, even in Likud circles, of the now generally accepted "two-state solution." This piece appeared in the *Jewish Herald* on 4 August 1988.

# ISRAEL'S DAY OF RECKONING IS AT HAND

In modern Hebrew the word "land" (eretz) is shorthand for "land of Israel". When you're abroad, you're "outside the land". I've been outside the land. Now I'm back – and the difference is startling.

I left Israel in April, the *intifada* at its height. After twenty years of complacency, with bipartisan "no peace, no war" policies, Israel has learnt that quiescence had never meant acquiescence. The calm had been revealed as the calm before the storm.

In April there were no new ideas around for tackling Palestinian aspirations or the future of the occupied territories. Early hopes that it would all be over by Christmas had proved – as so often – illusory. Especially shocking to many was the revelation that Teddy Kollek's

20-year achievement, his "united Jerusalem", seemed as fragile as the rest of the structure.

Kollek's Jerusalem had been living proof that Arab and Jew could live peacefully side by side, bound together by common interest. But one commercial strike and one night of rioting in East Jerusalem shattered the illusion.

Clearly, the political climate has changed. On the Palestinian side the new realism is typified by prominent West Banker, Hanna Siniora, editor of the newspaper *Al Fajr*. He declares unequivocally that the new Palestinian goal is no longer the destruction of Israel, but a two–state solution in which mutual recognition leads to peaceful coexistence. He foresees an economic confederation of Israel, Palestine and Jordan akin to that linking the Benelux countries, with enormous benefits to all – for Israel, access to the colossal 200 million–strong markets of the Arab world. Realistic Palestinians, he says, have abandoned their dream of recovering the whole of the land; realistic Israelis must do the same.

The same ideas are now emerging from the PLO. Leading Arafat adviser, Bassam Abu Sharif, recently declared that any bargain must guarantee Israel's security, thus supporting the two–state solution. As for Palestinian representation at the negotiations, he calls for a referendum in the occupied territories to select the delegation. Although denounced by hard–liners in the PLO, Sharif's statement has been welcomed within the territories.

Inside Israel the most liberal voice has come from where you would least expect it – the military establishment. The top brass most fearlessly supports compromise. Perhaps they best appreciate Israel's strategic requirements on the West Bank (which are far less than generally believed), and the danger in continuing an indefinite military occupation of a rebellious population.

And so we find senior Israeli Defense Force figures as founder members of a new Council for Peace and Security. Reserve General Shlomo Gazit asserts that Israel must give up most of the territories so that she can arrive at an agreement that the Arabs can live with. A tranche of other reserve generals – Menahem Meron, Amos Lapidot, Orri Orr – agree. Reserve General Yosef Geva sums up the aims of the Council as "to show the public that there is a legitimate view that recognises the need for, and the feasibility of, compromise." Coming from respected figures, scarcely indifferent about security, such views carry weight.

Among the ideas generated by the Council is actually negotiating with the PLO. This is the acid test of the new realism. The recent Arab summit made it clear that King Hussein is retreating fast from the idea of himself heading Arab negotiations on behalf of the Palestinians.

The inter–factional struggles within the PLO have again projected Yasser Arafat to the top of the pile where he now perches, albeit somewhat uneasily, since his relationship with Syria's President Assad, to say nothing of Egypt's Mubarak, remains equivocal.

Still, an Arafat–led PLO delegation, endorsed by the Arab states and supported by West Bank and Gaza Palestinians, seems now the obvious Palestinian representation in any negotiations. But within Israel, Likud and Labour Alignment remain as resolutely opposed to sitting down with the PLO as most Labour and Tory politicians in Britain would abhor the idea of negotiating a British withdrawal from Northern Ireland face to face with the leaders of the IRA.

Shared sovereignty is one policy. Proposals take many shapes. Israel's strategic requirements might be adequately safeguarded, it is argued, by granting restricted rights in a West Bank forming part of a Palestinian state. The *quid pro quo* could be concessions on citizenship to Arabs resident in Israel.

Or, Jews of the West Bank might opt for Israeli citizenship while Arabs in Israel could choose to become citizens of Palestine.

All these options are founded on a recent strategic reappraisal for Israel of the West Bank, again spearheaded by the military. Former Israeli air force commander Amos Lapidot is on the record as saying that, with early warning radar and an air defense capability, most of the land is of little strategic value. It is controlling the West Bank air space that concerns him.

Reserve brigadier–general Ephraim Sneh, once head of the West Bank's civil administration, believes that three airborne warning and control system aircraft (AWACs) would provide better early warning than the entire network of ground–based stations now sited in the mountain areas of the West Bank. Others – notably reserve Brigadier–General Aryeh Shaley – are less inclined to put so many eggs in the airborne system basket. Such fundamental speculation leads to a growing recognition that while Israel may have real, albeit strictly limited, strategic interests in the West Bank, they are not necessarily incompatible with a "land for peace" settlement.

Are the elements of a viable settlement floating about in this primaeval broth? If so, a formidable catalyst is required. Where is it to come from? The Israeli general election, due on 1 November, will focus the issues, but much will turn on how far thinking the unthinkable has by then changed the electorate.

*The Jewish Herald*
*4 August 1988*

\*

Involved as I was, through various aspects of my working life, in both public relations and in radio, I was always especially interested in the way Israel presented itself to the outside world. I still am, come to that. During 1989 a fascinating debate began in the pages of the *Jewish Chronicle* about the need for Israel to become considerably more professional in the way it addressed the outside world, and considerably more concerned about the image it was creating in the public perception. I joined the debate, first in the letter pages of the *Jewish Chronicle*. This contribution appeared in the issue of 1st of September 1989.

The Editor
The Jewish Chronicle.

Sir,

In outlining a solution to Israel's endemic public relations problem (August 25), David Davis has the right idea – an organisation geared to the local presentation of Israel's case.

An influx of British PR people, however expert, who were simply skilled in serving the needs of the British media, is no answer.

Everyone in the media world knows that, as they step foot on the tarmac at Ben–Gurion airport, they must undertake an essential, sometimes painful, readjustment of perspective (it becomes easier with time). The world viewed from Jerusalem has its own order of priorities, very different from the familiar London-based aspect. I have learned this lesson in agonised discussion with Israeli media friends.

It seemed only too clear, I told them, that no one was taking sufficient, if any, interest in how the British media perceived Israel's actions, nor in explaining her problems and policies in a way designed to elicit understanding among the British public. In return, and gently, I have learned that what the British media does, and what the British public think, come some way down the ranking.

To people working in Kol Yisrael's external radio services, for example, greatly concerned as they are with Israel's image abroad, the top priority is the USA, with the USSR a close second. South Africa, with its important Jewish population, West Germany and even Canada, probably rank above Britain in the pecking order. We have some importance, but we are not top dog.

Our major concern in this country, of course, is to achieve a better presentation of Israel in general. The presentational skills necessary to achieve this are, however, very different from those required to do the same job in Georgia, USA, or in Georgia, USSR. This is why any coordinated approach to the problem must involve establishing a PR operation that is capable of interpreting Israel's position in terms that are appropriate, and make sense, to the particular audiences being addressed.

British PR expertise may certainly be of assistance in this; it cannot provide the whole answer.

Yours, etc

*1 September 1989*

\*

I followed this up with a letter to the *Jerusalem Post*. It appeared on the 4th of October 1989, and was reprinted in the International Edition the following month.

The Editor
The Jerusalem Post

Sir,

A debate is being conducted in the pages of Britain's leading Jewish weekly, *The Jewish Chronicle*, about ways of improving the presentation of Israel's image to the world. Three leading British public relations experts were agreed in drawing attention to Israel's obvious failure to treat public relations with the seriousness it merits. PR today, it was pointed out, is a highly skilled professional activity; bungling amateurs usually do more harm than good. Some suggested that a sort of task force of British PR people should he placed at Israel's disposal.

I entered the debate to point out that, while British PR expertise could certainly help, it could not provide the whole answer. The essence of effective PR is to tailor the presentation of a case to suit the intended audience. Skill, however great, in preparing material for the British media would be of little use to do the same job effectively in, say, Georgia USA or Georgia USSR.

British ears, for example, to an extent rarely understood abroad, are sensitively attuned to accent and delivery. In Professor Higgins, Shaw struck a rich seam in the British make-up. Not only is class instantly identified through accent but, more importantly, credibility by the mode of delivery. President Herzog or Abba Eban invariably carry conviction on the British broadcast media; an American accent bears with it a host of alien, albeit not unfriendly connotations; an Israeli accent, especially coupled with normal Israeli ways of saying things, often simply spells "Foreigner – beware."

The USSR has, of course, recognized this for a number of years now by providing the British broadcast media with fluent, convincing spokesmen speaking unaccented standard English. I would suggest that the best thing Israel can do, as a start towards achieving an effective national public relations operation, would be to establish, for both the broadcast and the printed media, teams of appropriately trained professionals, geared to presenting current affairs issues to the parts of the world that matter, in ways that really carry conviction.

Yours etc

*4 October 1989*

\*

I have always taken a keen interest in Kol Yisrael, "The Voice of Israel" – Israel's national radio organisation – and especially in its external services, then mainly broadcasting on short-wave channels. Towards the end of 1989 I was invited into Kol Yisrael's external service studios, and spoke to many of those responsible for running the service.

# ISRAEL SPEAKS TO THE WORLD

Slowly the second–hand hops up the steep hill towards the hour, and suddenly the silence of the control room is shattered by the first pip of the time signal. On the dot of the hour the studio manager clicks on a pre–recorded tape, and over a few bars of introductory music comes the station announcement:

"This is Kol Yisrael, the voice of Israel, broadcasting from Jerusalem."

On the other side of a large glass panel Zvi Pantanowicz, veteran English service newscaster and senior producer, launches into the bulletin.

It is 1 p.m. in Israel, and the news is being broadcast throughout the country for the benefit of English speakers. But for listeners in Australia it is Israel's mid–evening bulletin; for New York it is the early morning newscast; in Britain it is 11 a.m. For as Pantanowicz speaks in Kol Yisrael's radio headquarters in the Romema district of Jerusalem, his words are borne instantaneously to a short–wave centre just outside Tel Aviv, where powerful transmitters ensure that Israel's voice is heard loud and clear across the world.

"Today, by common consent," says Victor Grajewski, director of Israel Radio International, "Israel is counted among the top ten inter-national broadcasting organisations – and not far below middle–rank-ing at that. We hold our place in terms of coverage, audibility and influence – quite an achievement for a country as small as Israel."

Kol Yisrael's achievements in international broadcasting – 1990 marks the 40th anniversary – emerge when the first external services director, British–born Dr Geoffrey Wigoder, reminisces.

Domestic broadcasting in British–mandated Palestine began in 1936, but there was no tradition of external broadcasting for Kol Yisrael to build on after independence. The initiative came from the World Zionist Organisation. A 1949 agreement signed by Ben–Gurion for the government provided the Jewish Agency with the rights to broadcast overseas from Israel. In return, the WZO met the cost of erecting transmitters, recruiting staff and acquiring studios and equipment.

"Kol Zion Lagola" ("The Voice of Zion to the Diaspora"), as the service was called, went on air in March 1950 with an inaugural message from Chaim Weizmann.

"When we began," says Wigoder, "our output consisted of brief daily transmissions in only three languages besides Hebrew – Yiddish, French and English."

The process of strengthening and extending the service began almost at once. An early development was the Transcription Service, begun in 1951 to send recorded programmes to overseas radio stations.

Today Hannah Lieblein heads an operation regularly supplying more than a thousand stations world–wide with recorded programmes in a welter of languages. In Britain both BBC and IBA local stations take Kol Yisrael's weekly output, which includes a 30–minute "Israel Magazine" and a Letter from Israel.

The current organisation of Kol Yisrael's external broadcasting seems like a stepping–stone to some future rationalisation.

Victor Grajewski's Israel Radio International, the direct descendant of Kol Zion Lagola, is structured in five directorates which, on the face of it, seem to cover the whole spectrum of Kol Yisrael's non–domestic services. However organisations, like the people who compose them, are full of inconsistencies.

Take radio news. While Zvi Pantanowicz was reading the 1 p.m. bulletin, the head of English news, ex–Londoner Harley Braidman, explained the set–up.

The English and French news services are, by a decision taken some years ago, incorporated into the domestic news division of Kol Yisrael, and thus fall outside Israel Radio International. Housed in the elegantly refurbished radio centre in Romema, Israel radio's integrated news division functions from a cleverly–designed suite of offices and studios, now firmly nicknamed "Mecca". From a spacious central control area, offices and studios radiate outwards, while great double–glass panels provide sight–lines through and between the many units.

As part of radio news division, Braidman and his team have direct access to the flood of raw news that pours into the centre in a continual torrent, day and night. He and his French counterpart participate in the morning news conference, attended also by domestic Hebrew service editorial controllers and producers, where the general pattern of news presentation for the day is decided. The framework agreed, Braidman and his team have complete editorial freedom to present the news to English–speaking listeners as they see fit.

Six English bulletins are transmitted each day, three carried exclusively on short wavebands to various parts of the world, three – like the 1 p.m. bulletin – also broadcast on a domestic channel in Israel.

Braidman agreed that the arrangement is something less than perfect. The news requirements of overseas listeners vary country by country; they certainly differ, sometimes quite markedly, from the needs of people living in Israel. Simultaneous transmission means compromise on what could ideally be achieved by way of a full service to Kol Yisrael's many English–speaking listeners.

"If the resources were available," says Braidman, "which unfortunately they are not, I would if necessary have two separate English bulletins going out at the same time – one written with domestic, and the other with overseas, listeners in mind."

Not that he feels the current arrangements mean any compromise in the standards of accuracy and objectivity laid down in Kol Yisrael's codex, and rigidly adhered to.

"Our reputation in the field of international broadcasting," says Braidman, "is largely based on a general recognition that we live up to the highest standards in our news reporting."

Simultaneous transmission poses no great problem to Moshe Sela, head of the Western World division of Israel Radio International.

"Our radio features," says Sela, "are usually just as relevant to home as to overseas listeners."

Sara Manobla, Newcastle–born head of English language pro-grammes, agrees. Her service spreads its net wide. Regular features cover press reviews, literature and the performing arts, living and travelling in Israel, a chat show, a mail–box programme, Israeli music of all kinds and the Jewish religion. She welcomes the chance to address English speakers within Israel as well as Kol Yisrael's vast English–speaking audience world–wide.

How large is that global audience? Using the computation based on letters received, now adopted generally by international broadcast-ing organisations, Victor Grajewski estimates it conservatively as 12 million regular listeners to the English service, and of the order of 20 million to Israel Radio International as a whole.

The simultaneous transmission issue is not relevant to the rest of the overseas output. English and French aside, programmes in the other 16 languages, news bulletins included, emanate from within the directorate.

"We receive the domestic Hebrew language bulletins from Romema during the day," explains Moshe Sela, "and each section translates and adapts them to suit its own listeners."

Where in the spectrum of Kol Yisrael's external activities do its broadcasts to the Arab world come? Another apparent anomaly.

"Kol Yisrael's Arabic service," explains its director, Iraqi–born Edmund Sehayek, "is quite separate from both the domestic and the International divisions. We became a free–standing operation in 1978, and I report direct to the Director–General of the Israel Broadcasting Authority.'"

On a variety of medium and short wavebands – one of the transmitters a 1200 Kw giant – Israel is in continuous contact both with its own Arabic speaking citizens and with each of its Arab neighbours.

Sehayek explains that the Arabic service has, perhaps surprisingly, built up a reputation among its listeners both domestic and foreign for accurate and objective news reporting far exceeding that of competitive stations – apart, possibly, from the BBC and the Voice of America. Egypt is the only Arab country to have carried out an effective listener survey. There, Kol Yisrael's Arabic service, with 7 million regular listeners, comes second only to Radio Monte Carlo as the foreign station listened to most often.

As far as Israel itself and the territories are concerned, explains Sehayek, the Arabic service achieves extremely high coverage because it has come to be regarded as infinitely superior to competitive stations in its music and general interest programmes and, in terms of news and comment, its speed, accuracy and objectivity.

"We are engaged in a war of information," says Sehayek, "and we have earned the trust of listeners. A measure of our effect on Arab public opinion is the extent to which neighbouring Arab countries continually refer to our broadcasts."

Another is listener response. Five thousand letters a month reach the Arabic service, many through a circuitous route established via a Post Office Box in Geneva, others direct from Egypt or through the territories. One radio feature in particular generates an enormous reaction – a twice–weekly medical advice programme presented for many years by Iraqi–born Elana Basri. Listeners, many from hard–line Arab countries, go to extraordinary lengths to be treated by the Israeli doctors who appear in the broadcasts, or in the Israeli hospitals mentioned in the programmes.

Where the Arabic service had to fight for acceptance by a basically hostile audience, broadcasts to the Jews of the USSR over the years have been directed to people desperately eager to hear the programmes, however persistent the jamming.

"If I had to pick out what has given me most satisfaction," says Victor Grajewski, "it is our Russian broadcasts. The evidence of their value in fostering a sense of Jewish identity grows daily with the rising tide of Russian immigration. We have already had hundreds of new Russian immigrants writing or coming to see us to say 'thank you' for our broadcasts over the past 20 years."

The thaw in eastern Europe has had other spin–offs for Kol Yisrael. Shortly after the restoration of diplomatic ties between Israel and Hungary, the two broadcasting organisations signed an agreement which has led to a major cultural exchange this autumn.

An Hungarian week on Israel radio is to be followed by an Israeli week on Hungary's domestic radio network. The event ensures unprecedented exposure for Hebrew literature, poetry and drama in an eastern European country. Ephraim Sten, head of Kol Yisrael's Arts Department, will be directing radio plays by three Israeli dramatists in the Budapest radio studios. Poets – five of Jewish origin – contacted by Literary Department head, Dr Shmuel Huppert, during a visit to Hungary earlier this year, will have their work broadcast in Israel. This exchange seals the "diplomacy of poets", fostered even before the formal restoration of relations, by people like Itamar Yaoskest, who translated an anthology of Hungarian poetry into Hebrew, and Andrash Mezei, the Hungarian Jewish poet, who has over the past few years introduced Hebrew poetry to Hungary.

Kol Yisrael has been notably successful in maintaining old ties and building new ones through the medium of radio. Fostered and developed, the external broadcasting services could, on the evidence, be one of the ways open to Israel in the future to win more friends and influence more people.

No sooner, it seemed, had I put my pen down, than came the astonishing announcement that the Israel Broadcasting Authority had decided on savage cut-backs in its external radio transmissions. To me, this seemed a bizarrely short-sighted policy. The *Jerusalem Post* published my anguished reaction on the 17th of June 1991.

The Editor,
The Jerusalem Post

Sir,

I was very saddened to read your editorial of June 5 approving – or, at any rate, not disapproving – the IBA's decision to reduce drastically its foreign broadcasts. The grounds quoted – lack of rigorous scientific audience statistics – are as specious as the hoped-for economy is false.

Short of commissioning market research in each of the countries targeted – a hugely expensive operation not even, I understand, undertaken regularly by the Voice of America – the methods of measuring radio listenership generally accepted in broadcasting circles point to Kol Yisrael's external services as standing extremely high in the league of world broadcasters, certainly among the "top ten". These methods are based on a correlation between average unsolicited mail receipts and the potential listening "universe" in each of the targeted areas. The IBA must be aware of this.

It has always been vitally important for Israel's voice to be heard loud and clear across the world – and never more so than now. The benefits to Israel's image abroad are incalculable. People resident here in Israel might be surprised at how often Israel radio is quoted in the BBC's domestic news broadcasts, and on particularly momentous occasions, by way of a recording taken direct from the English-language broadcasts of Kol Yisrael. The only other external broadcasting service treated in this way is Radio Moscow's World Service.

Broadcasting is one field in which Israel can successfully compete with the rest of the world in the battle for the sympathy and understanding of ordinary people. Radio is so comparatively cheap that it seems the height of folly to cast aside a reputation – to say nothing of the expertise – built up by 25 years of dedicated broadcasters in the external services to a world-wide audience almost certainly not less in total than 20 million people.

Rather, as you tentatively suggest, attention should be directed to ways in which this invaluable asset of Israel could be further developed.

Yours etc.

*17 June 1991*

\*

Inevitably the cuts went ahead, but something remained of the external service and they struggled on for another couple of years. Then came the *coup de grace*. The external services in English were to be slashed to virtual extinction. All that would remain would be a few basic news broadcasts. Was there ever a clearer case of cutting off one's nose to spite one's face? *The Jerusalem Post* published this letter from me on the 8th of January, 1995.

The Editor
The Jerusalem Post.

Sir,

The premier language of international communications is English. If Israel is to present itself to the world effectively, win friends and influence people, it must give high – and possibly top – priority to talking to the world in English.

How profoundly depressing, therefore, to read in your issue of December 26 that Kol Yisrael's overseas broadcasts in English are to be slashed for the sake of putative "savings" of a few hundred thousand dollars. Heaven knows, there is a lack of understanding about Israel, its people, its points of view, its cultural life. More than ever, Israel needs to be talking confidently to the rest of the world through its shortwave broadcasts – a wonderful range of programs, especially those in English which reach the US, Canada, the UK, Europe, South Africa and Australia.

Rather than cutting back on these transmissions, I urge the government and Kol Yisrael to set up a working party to see how quickly they can be expanded to be carried via satellite for cable retransmission overseas, and how quickly Kol Yisrael can exploit the forthcoming new technology of digital audio broadcasting (DAB).

Yours, etc

*8 January 1995*

\*

That week I wrote also to the *Jewish Chronicle*. My letter appeared in the issue of 13 January 1995. It need hardly be said that neither letter did the slightest bit of good, and the announced cuts took place. As from 1996 the English language service of Kol Yisrael, with its wide range of political, cultural, literary and music programmes, was dead.

The Editor
The Jewish Chronicle.

Sir,

Regular listeners to Israel Radio's short-wave broadcasts in English will no doubt be feeling as profoundly depressed as I at the announcement that, as from January 1, the time allocated to these transmissions has been savagely reduced. Two regular half-hour programmes have been removed from the schedules, leaving only 75 minutes of English-language broadcasting each day.

For the sake of putative "savings" of a few hundred thousand dollars, Kol Yisrael is gagging Israel's voice in what is the premier language of international communications. More than ever, Israel needs to be talking confidently to the rest of the world through its short-wave broadcasts. Far from cutting back, Israel ought to be considering how they can be expanded and how quickly Kol Yisrael can exploit the new technology of digital audio broadcasting.

Yours, etc.

*13 January 1995*

\*

# THE PASSING SCENE - 4

It's odd how large a part radio plays in daily life in Israel. Walk down any suburban street from the Golan to Eilat, and the time signal pursues you from window to window. All the buses, of course, are equipped with radios, and come news time the driver invariably turns up the volume so all the passengers can catch the bulletin.

"A legacy," a confiding fellow passenger told me, "of the early days of the State when our very existence literally depended, hour to hour, on what was happening on our borders."

The obsession with the radio news persists. But the five radio channels now available throughout Israel also offer a wide variety of entertainment. The "Voice of Music" channel provides classical music throughout the day. The other channels are more mixed, however, with a variety of light and popular music, features and radio drama.

I spent a fascinating few hours with Eran Baniel, head of radio drama for the Israel Broadcasting Authority. Operating with sadly restricted facilities, in terms of both manpower and equipment, Eran has built an international reputation for the IBA in radio circles. As a distinguished radio man himself, but also as a director for the Habima Theatre – the nearest equivalent to a National Theatre in Israel – he has for several years acted as one of the judges for the Prix Italia, the prestigious radio awards scheme. Now he has been invited to undertake a production himself for BBC Radio next spring to mark the 40th anniversary of the founding of the State of Israel. It should be on the air in April, so watch out for it!

*

When people first go to Israel, they find a country whose infrastructure is so well–developed that they automatically expect life to be very similar to what they are used to at home. In many respects it is.

Some of the differences are perfectly understandable, given the geography and the climate. Others take a little getting used to.

Daily doorstep deliveries of milk, for example – so familiar to us – could hardly be a feature of everyday life in an eastern Mediterranean country. With the sun beating down at up to 100 degrees for eight months of the year in many places, the idea of a milk float ambling round the streets, milk bottles standing on doorsteps for hours, is patently absurd.

So Israelis buy their milk from the chilled cabinets in the local "super". But not, I hasten to say, in bottles – either of glass or the plastic type. It comes in horrid, squirmy, clammy, damp plastic bags, yes bags, that have to have their corners nipped off.

Almost every kitchen possesses several of the special rigid containers into which you are supposed to place your milk bag before snipping off its corner.

Do remember, otherwise you are likely to find yourself and your kitchen floor covered in milk.

If Israelis are worse off than we Britons regarding milk, they score mightily when it comes to the collection of rubbish. Again, it's the climate that provides the rationale. Wait a week for each visit of the dustman, as is the norm in England, and most Israeli homes would be unapproachable. So the general rule in Israel is a thrice–weekly collection of rubbish. Most apartment blocks and houses have a structure adjacent to the building to house the dustbins, which are usually emptied on Sundays, Tuesdays and Thursdays – normally before midday. It is all a highly efficient operation and could, I am sure, be studied with advantage by the entrepreneurs who are nowadays bidding for our own local authority garbage collection services.

Now, let us consider the mail. Yes of course letters are delivered to the door in Israel, and so are postcards (well, not quite to the door, but I'll explain that shortly). But you will look in vain for anything approaching a consistent parcel delivery service. I believe that, in theory, postmen are expected to make one attempt to deliver packages up to a certain size. In fact, in my experience, none are delivered. Instead, the postman will leave a note in your mail box to say a parcel awaits collection at your local post office.

I say "mail box" because this North American practice is virtually universal in Israel. Front doors in Israel do not come equipped with letter boxes, English–style. Your Israeli postman expects to find a sequence of numbered mail boxes at the entrance of each block of apartments – and an individual box on a pole adjacent to the front gate of each house.

The boxes provided in most apartment blocks are, moreover, so poky and inconvenient that it is sometimes difficult even to insert a rolled–up magazine. Packages of any sort would be an impossibility. Hence the *poste restante* system.

Go into any local post office in Israel, and you will find a special counter at which to collect your parcels and packages. Behind the clerk, you will invariably see a huge amount of mail waiting to be collected. It's a fiendish system. The advice note your postman leaves you provides no kind of clue as to the size, let alone the weight, of the package awaiting collection. You could arrive with a wheelbarrow only to be handed a tiny box containing a slice of wedding cake, or you could roll up all unsuspecting to be lumbered with a vast box that will necessitate taking a taxi home. As someone once said: "There must be a better way."

How pampered we are in this country for newspapers. You don't realise the ultimate luxury of receiving a daily paper on your doormat ·in time for breakfast, come rain or shine – until it is not there.

In Israel you can rely on this particular luxury only when you stay in the better class hotels, which make a point of wishing you "good morning" with a copy of the *Jerusalem Post*. Otherwise, it's a trek down to the local shops.

Now here, it has always seemed to me, is a business opportunity ripe for the grabbing. Surely some enterprising newspaper retailer has only to offer the Israeli public a doorstep delivery service, for his fortune to be made.

Or would it? There's an old saying: "What you've never had, you never miss," so, perhaps the demand would have to be created rather than simply exploited. All the same, there would surely be many subscribers, even if, since their front doors have no letter boxes for their newpaper to be shoved through, Israelis would be reduced to picking it off their front door mat each morning.

Anyone planning aliyah and looking for a way to make a living? Think about it!

*

Israel is, of course, replete with history – layers of it. The names of the towns and cities usually recall Biblical times, the streets have often been named for more recent events and heroes.

In Jerusalem, for example, Herzog and Herzl and Weizmann are commemorated, along with our own King George V, in whose reign the Balfour Declaration was signed.

In Tel Aviv you will find another street named for King George V, and others for the poet Bialik, and Ben–Gurion, and General Allenby, who liberated Palestine from the Turks.

Haifa, too, honours Allenby and Herzl, and has a major boulevard dedicated to the memory of the Haganah. It also has room for Wingate and Balfour and Wedgwood – the British connection, as you will note, is strong.

You are usually left to make the historical connections yourself by asking, or by buying one of the tourist guides. It is rare for the visitor to be given the background to a particular place name. Visit the Kikar Denya in the Bet Ha'Kerem suburb of Jerusalem, though, and you will find the whole story laid out for you.

Kikar Denya translates as Denmark Circus. It is a large open space, forming a natural focus for the neighbourhood. Trees and bushes are planted all around, and some trees advance into the open space itself, providing welcome shade for the old people and mothers with prams who rest on the many benches.

A large and impressive piece of modern sculpture adorns the kikar. To one side, the visitor's attention must be drawn to a long plaque, inscribed with a message in five languages: Danish, Swedish. English, Arabic and Hebrew. This is what it says:

*"In October 1943, the Danish people and Resistance Movement defied the Nazi occupation of their country to rescue their Jewish fellow citizens. During ten nights, almost all Danish Jewry – over 7,000 people – were spirited across the Oeresund in fishing boats and other small craft to safety in Sweden. Danish courage and Swedish generosity gave indelible proof of human values in times of barbarism. Israel and Jews everywhere will never forget."*

\*

Took a trip down into the Negev – the vast V–shaped desert area that narrows down to the single point of Eilat at Israel's southernmost tip. The objective: David Ben–Gurion's home from 1953 until he died – the kibbutz of Sede Boqer.

Driving down into the desert is a fascinating experience, unlike anything else in the world. The first part of the journey south from Jerusalem takes you past isolated Arab farms, most of which seem very green and prosperous. Then you arrive at the thriving desert city of Beer-Sheva, Israel's fourth largest city.

Two contrasting experiences not to be missed: a wander round the large, bustling Arab market full to overflowing with produce from the very farms you have just passed; and relaxing in the blessed air-conditioning of one of the luxury hotels.

However, you will find that no matter where you are in Beer-Sheva, the close proximity of the desert impinges on your consciousness. And indeed, just a few minutes' drive down Sderot David Tuviyahu, and the desert embraces you – the real desert, this time, with its vast distances and its silence. And the silence of the desert – not a bird, not a breath of wind, nothing – has to be experienced to be believed.

Drive 40 kilometres further south, and the road brings you to Sede Boqer. Cars are directed off the main road into the kibbutz proper, where Ben–Gurion's house is preserved for visitors to wander round. Walk back a few yards, and you arrive at the entrance to the area set aside to his memory. You are directed through a beautifully land-scaped garden until, suddenly, you find yourself in a circular area, the edge of which falls away dramatically to reveal a vast desert plain that stretches to a far horizon.

Within the circular area lie the graves of David and Paula Ben–Gurion, with their simple tombstones. No more moving, or more appropriate, setting for one of Israel's founding fathers, could have been conceived.

*

This experience came vividly to mind when, in 1990, a letter in the *Jewish Chronicle* suggested that the Galilee might be a suitable substitute for the West Bank, as a development area for the immigrants expected to descend in droves on Israel following the collapse of the Soviet Union – as indeed they did. My letter in response was published in the *Jewish Chronicle* of the 9th of February 1990.

The Editor
The Jewish Chronicle

Sir,

Mr Freedman (February 2) considers the Galilee an area ripe for further development and suggests that Mr Shamir direct his attention northward rather than to the West Bank if he is seeking *lebensraum* for the expected influx of Soviet immigrants.

While not disagreeing with Mr Freedman, I might, if I had five minutes of Mr Shamir's time on this matter, choose rather to direct his attention to an unshakable tenet of the political faith of one of Israel's founding fathers – David Ben-Gurion.

Aware that some three-quarters of Israel's land mass is taken up by the Negev, Ben-Gurion was passionately convinced that, for the sake of its own future, Israel must direct substantial resources at wresting a viable economy and way of life from the wilderness.

A visit to Ben-Gution's kibbutz home at Sde Boker reveals how far he engaged himself personally in the effort, and there have been substantial scientific, agronomical and social successes.

The results show in the continuous increase in the numbers of those choosing to live in the towns of the Negev, and in the economic, cultural and academic explosion that has taken place in Beer-Sheva, the regional centre, in the past few years.

Here in the Negev is where the old dream of "making the desert bloom" is a living reality – and it is a dream that would surely fire the imagination of a new generation of immigrants, just as it did their fathers.

Yours, etc.

*9 February 1990*

\*

On my first visits to Israel, it was natural enough for me, as a radio writer myself, to make contact with people engaged in radio, and that's how I first got to know Shmuel Huppert. He was the head of literary programmes for Kol Yisrael's domestic radio channels. Over the years my wife and I became close friends with Shmuel and his wife, Mimi, but it was only slowly that it emerged that Shmuel was a holocaust survivor. Born in Czechoslovakia, at the age of seven in 1943 he was imprisoned in Bergen-Belsen concentration camp with his mother, where he stayed till the end of the war. Then, through friends, they both managed to be included in a batch of Jews from Europe legally admitted to Israel, then still under the British mandate. Many years later, the Israel Museum in Jerusalem mounted an exhibition of holocaust memorabilia, and Shmuel was moved to express his feelings in a poem, written in Hebrew, which he called "The Suitcase". One day he showed it to me, and asked if I would like to translate it into English. Together we worked out precisely what each word signified – and, even more, the intention behind each word selected by Shmuel.

I then reconceived the poem into English. Translation from one language into another is difficult enough at the best of times. Translating poetry amplifies the difficulties a hundred-fold. English is so rich a language, that virtually every word carries a whole baggage-train of connotations, implications and connections. One example – Shmuel Huppert's title: "The Suitcase". But the poem was also about the circumstances in which Otto Schwarzkopf's suitcase happened to be in Jerusalem. So I chose as the title "The Case of Otto Schwarzkopf",

drawing on the pun possible in English by using the word "case".
Did I distort Shmuel's poetic intention by doing this – and by
making a score of similar choices in converting the poem into
English? He thought not, and I hope not.

The poem was first published in the *Jewish Chronicle*'s Literary
Supplement on 11 January 1991. Nearly three years later, I
submitted it to *The Independent*, which at that period published
a poem every day. "The Case of Otto Schwarzkopf" appeared
as the *Independent*'s "Daily Poem" in the issue of 14 September
1993.

A few weeks later, I was approached by a music publishing firm
asking whether Shmuel and I would agree to the poem being set
to music by Ralph McTell. An agreement was quickly reached,
and in 1995 Ralph McTell's new CD album, "Sand in Your Shoes"
duly appeared, with "The Case of Otto Schwarzkopf" featuring
as track 11.

*

# THE CASE OF OTTO SCHWARZKOPF
## By Shmuel Huppert

*English version by Neville Teller from the original Hebrew*

Your case
Otto Schwarzkopf
has reached Jerusalem.

In the leather A.L.L.1
branded black
and Otto Schwarzkopf
a Prague address.
On the back
a hotel sticker
mountains of the Tyrol
prayer-shawl draped
with snow
pine pierced blue skies
a lake you swam in?

You went up into the mountain
alone
or was it a family outing?

The case gapes wide
a soundless cry
they pause to gaze at it at you
Otto.

Where now your content?
Under-wear
towel toothbrush shirt socks
the works of Heinrich Heine.
Family snaps.

In the winter of forty-four
the German order
just take what you need
twenty kilos apiece
one suitcase each
you're off to the east
no fuss leave everything else to us.

Now it's here
on show
the handle
your palm warmed Otto
cold
iron clasps rust covered.

Reference your trip A.L.L.1
Theresienstadt to Auschwitz
transportation trucks as per specification
7 cows or 30 pigs or 120 Jews.

Your case
Otto Schwarzkopf
has made its way without you
to Jerusalem.

\*

By the start of 1991 the enormous impact on Israel of the inevitable great Russian *aliyah* was a fruitful subject for comment and speculation.

# THE RUSSIANS ARE COMING

A dumpy middle–aged woman stopped a few feet away from me in the fruit and veg section of our local supermarket and picked up a packet of carrots. She examined it intently. Puzzled either by the weight or the price, she asked me a question. Nothing very strange in that, except that she spoke in Russian.

I wasn't able to help her, but this is Jerusalem. In a few seconds she was surrounded by a group of helpful shoppers, and out of a babble containing discernible elements of Hebrew, Yiddish, English and German, I saw that a response in Russian was hitting the target.

How long had that woman and her family been in Israel? Almost certainly no more than a month or so, perhaps much less. She was living evidence of Israel's priority issue in these first weeks of 1991 – not the Gulf, not the intifada, vitally important to the country's future though both are, but immigration from the Soviet Union.

In 1989, some 25,000 Soviet Jews made their way to Israel. At the time, after years of repression and tough restrictions on emigration, it seemed like the opening of the floodgates. What is happening now can be encapsulated in a single statistic. The number of new immigrants arriving in Israel in the last week of 1990 alone just about equalled that for the whole of 1989.

Immigration from the Soviet Union grew steadily month by month last year, but the flow turned into a torrent in November and December. At one point planes loaded to capacity were landing from Eastern Europe at the rate of one every half–hour.

It was, dramatically enough, on the evening of 31st December that Igor Goldfarb, a 25–year–old engineer from Chivilisk in the Urals, stepped onto the tarmac at Ben Gurion airport with his 62–year–old mother, to a bewildering welcoming committee of TV cameras, Press photographers and two Ministers. He was, officially, the 200,000[th] immigrant of 1990.

The Government are planning to receive 400,000 in 1991. Proportionately, it is as though the UK had absorbed some 3 million new citizens last year, and expected a further 6 million this. Perhaps the strangest aspect of all this to an observer from the UK is that, in all the turmoil and hurly–burly of Israeli political life, where every issue, large and small, is hotly debated and opinions are fragmented almost to infinity, not a single voice seems to have been raised against the inflow. Many, varied and vociferous are the criticisms of the alleged inadequacies of the Government in dealing with the crisis, but no–one appears to be questioning the nation's obligation to receive – more, to welcome – the flood of new immigrants from Eastern Europe.

Reasons are not hard to find. A large proportion – perhaps the bulk – of Israel's 4 million Jewish population are themselves immigrants or the children of immigrants. The experience of being uprooted and trying to carve a new life in a strange environment is fresh in the consciousness. More to the point, every Israeli imbibes from birth the *ralson d'être* of the State – to provide a national home for the Jewish people and to promote the in–gathering of the exiles.

So, while accusations of ineptitude and lack of foresight are shuttlecocked between Absorption Minister Peretz and Housing Minister Sharon, and they fight public battles over their favoured instant remedies to the problem – like importing vast quantities of caravans (Sharon) or tents (Peretz) – and while the media peddle magic bullet remedies, like converting all the unused hotel rooms into b–and–b accommodation (Israel is suffering from an unprecedented collapse of tourism in the wake of the Gulf crisis), the nation is getting on with the business of adapting itself to massive change.

The signs are everywhere. The airport coaches that shuttle passengers between plane and terminal now have large illuminated advertisements in Hebrew, English and Russian urging new arrivals to use the services of Bank Leumi. Notices in Russian are sprouting in high street shop windows everywhere. The TV news headlines at 8 pm each evening carry subtitles in Russian. Even the illustrated ABC book I bought the kids last week presents the alphabet in the Hebrew, Latin and Cyrillic scripts.

What are the deeper implications of all this? It seems pretty clear that what is a comparatively minor backwash generated by the ebbing tide of European communism has plunged Israel into one of the key episodes in her history.

The old certainties are dissolving. Not long ago received opinion saw a continuing and inexorable swing in the internal demographic balance away from the European Ashkenazi element – which provided virtually all the founding fathers of the State – towards the Sephardi, drawn from the poorer Jewish immigrants from the countries of the Middle East. Born and bred in Arab societies and conversant with Arab culture, these Sephardi Jews almost invariably favour a tough political stance in the eternal Arab–Israel conflict, and the present Likud government draws a great deal of its support from them. The balance is shifting before our eyes back in favour of the Ashkenazi. The political complexion of future Israeli governments will turn on how these new citizens choose to exercise their franchise.

Two million or more new European immigrants – even if, as appears to be happening, they are virtually all accommodated in Israel proper and not on the West Bank – also changes what was accepted wisdom on the Arab-Jewish demographic balance. Until quite recently it has been possible to chart the point at which the much higher birth-rate among the Arab population would convert Israel's Arab minority into a majority. Israel's statisticians will have to think again.

So will the strategists and economists. How far will Israel be strengthened by the influx in terms of defensive capability? How far will the native abilities, skills and talents of Israel's new citizens enhance national life and bring what are at present unmeasurable benefits to their newly adopted country?

Israel's future, just like America's in the last century, is being shaped by a great wave of the indigent and oppressed fleeing from their own countries to seek a new life in a new land. Meanwhile, the two great international issues which will equally shape the future hang in the balance – peace or war in the Gulf, and the future of the dispossessed Palestinians.

*

Time for another story. This one came to mind as I was thinking one day of pre-intifada times, when one could wander at will through the shouk in the old city of Jerusalem. Entering, perhaps, by the Jaffa gate, you would make your way through the narrow streets until you came to the bustling Arab market area, lined on both sides with shops selling every kind of product from hand-woven carpets and leather goods to the latest radios, hi-fis and fridges. The feeling I sought to convey in the story was the feeling I always get on reading that episode in James Hilton's "Lost Horizon", when the dying High Lama hands Shangri-La on to the hero, Conway. Did I succeed?

*

# THE LOVE OF BOOKS

It was, I remember, late in December, many years ago, at the time of day when evening is coming on but it is still not dark enough for the lights to be lit, that my husband Roni and I were wandering – as we often did in those early years of our marriage, before the children came – through the alleyways of old Jerusalem. At length we came to a short passage–way which opened out into a tiny court. We looked about us.

To left and right the crumbling frontages of two houses, vaguely oriental in appearance, eyed each other blankly through grimy uncurtained windows. And in one corner I thought I could detect an unexpected sight.

"Over there," I said, "isn't that a booksnop?"

"Ruth my love," said Roni, "you could smell out a bookshop at a thousand metres blindfolded! I'll bet you're right."

"And you, Roni my darling, could be trusted to take a bet on whether tomorrow will be Wednesday or not. Come on, let's go over and see."

We emerged from the passage–way, and the sounds of the old city faded behind us. Deep calm pervaded the courtyard – extraordinary when one remembered the frenzied activity only a short distance behind. As we made our way towards the far corner, the feeling of remoteness from everyday life was intensified. I was gripped by the strange sensation that time itself had somehow been suspended. I glanced at Roni, but he seemed quite unaffected, and was his usual insouciant self, mildly interested, half bored.

At length we stood before the tiny shop front. A faded facade proclaimed "LABAC – ANTIQUARIAN BOOKS". My nose close to the dusty glass, I peered in. I tried the door. For a moment it stuck, and I thought it was locked.

But it gave beneath my pressure.

The fading daylight seemed to extend only a short distance beyond the front door. The frontage was narrow, and both walls were lined from top to bottom with books, but the shop was so high that as the shelves rose upwards they faded into the shadows. The effect of books extending into infinity was even stronger as I peered into the interior, a narrowing cone of booklined darkness.

I looked about.

"Where do you think the owner is?"

"I am over here, madame."

The words were uttered in a precise, rather high–pitched voice with a pronounced French accent. I turned my head sharply. A stooped figure emerged from the shadows. White–haired, with a small goatee beard, and with half–moon spectacles perched on the end of his nose, the man seemed to personify the spirit of scholarship.

"Come in a little way," he said. "And you, sir."

I closed the door.

"Thank you, Mr...?"

"*Monsieur* Labac," said the old man. "I prefer 'Monsieur'. My family spent many hundreds of years in France before I made my way to Israel. I am too old now to want to change the customs of a lifetime."

He peered at me.

"Forgive an old man's eccentricities, but whenever I can like to know who I am dealing with. Anonymity I hate, above all things."

"I am Ruth Illyon," I said. "This is my husband, Roni."

"Pleased to make your acquaintance," said the old man. "And now, what can I do for you?"

"The truth," said Roni, "is that my wife is bewitched by books. She collects them as other people collect postage stamps. She finds it almost impossible to pass by a bookshop. Philosophers – that's her special delight."

The old man turned to me

"My dear, your husband thinks he tells me one thing about you. In fact he tells me two."

"How do you mean?"

"He tells me that you love books for themselves, and he tells me that you love what books contain. Believe me, Mrs Illyon, the two do not always go together."

The old man's eyes rested on me, and it seemed as if somewhere deep in my mind a key turned and a door opened.

"I know what you mean," I said, and suddenly I did. "For some people it is enough to hold an old book in their hands, to sniff the musty binding, to experience the sensual pleasure of running their fingers over the ancient paper or parchment, to caress the leather covers. The thoughts, ideas, stories, that are stored on those pages – this, to them, is of minor significance. For others, the content is all. The mystery, the excitement, the magic, is that the mind of one individual, long since dead, can through the medium of the printed page communicate over the centuries with one's own. Thoughts – mere ideas that float in the brain like seeds on the wind – have been captured and transferred across hundreds of years, from one mind to another. What does the physical form of the message matter to people like that?"

"But for you, my dear," said Monsieur Labac, "the two mysteries merge and become one. Am I right?"

"I must admit it."

"And you, Mr Illyon, do you share your wife's obsessions?"

Roni grinned.

"Afraid not, Monsieur Labac. I like the occasional gamble, that's all."

"I've been looking at these two books, Monsieur Labac," I said. "They seem very ancient."

"One is, and one is not. As you see, both are entitled *The Book of the Cabal*. The original... this... well, this is priceless. In one of the big auction houses in London or New York it could fetch millions. But see – a very clever publisher about a hundred years ago actually reproduced the effect of this ancient volume and some of the material. Here..."

It was skilfully done. The effect of the original had been cunningly recreated, down to the faded ink, the ragged edges to the pages, even the worn binding.

"What is the book?" I asked.

"The original is connected with one of the most closely guarded aspects of ancient Jewish philosophy. You know of the Caballah, Mrs Illyon?"

"Not very much, " I admitted.

The old man's delicate hands rested on one of the tomes.

"Locked into the five sacred books of the Torah is the mystery of the universe. Over the centuries a few gifted and privileged scholars have given their lives to wrestling with the texts, using the unique discipline of the Cabal. On the way they have unlocked many doors, but the final key still eludes them. This volume – and the clever reproduction of it – records part of that long journey of discovery."

"The reproduction," I said. ""It's so beautiful. Dare I ask how much it costs?"

Roni groaned.

"Mrs Illyon," said the old man, "believe me when I tell you that this is one book that I would not on any account sell to someone I thought unworthy of it. You I think worthy. I will sell it to you for... fifty dollars."

"Oh no," I said. "That can't be right. It must be worth more than that."

"Value," said Monsieur Labac, "like beauty, is in the eye of the beholder. To me the receipt of fifty dollars, together with the knowledge that the book is passing into your hands, Mrs Illyon, makes the transaction a bargain in my eyes. Believe me, it is so."

"Then of course I will take the book," I said. "You will accept a cheque?"

"But of course."

"Lend me your pen, Roni."

"Tell me, Monsieur Labac," said Roni, as he handed it over, "the Caballah – is it confined to the mysteries of the universe, or does it also tackle human existence?"

"There are caballists and caballists," said the old man. "A few have bent their minds to the question of where the division lies between discerning what is written on the page of the future, and actually inscribing a word or two on that page – between predicting and pre–ordaining events."

"But surely," I protested, "there's all the difference in the world."

"Not so, madame. If you assert that, you deny one of the fundamental principles of humanity's contract with the Almighty – free will. However powerful a caballist may be in bending future events to his desires, each individual involved will preserve to .the last instant his own freedom of decision – a freedom he can exercise to frustrate the desired end."

He stopped suddenly.

"There, I've spoken too much already. And it's getting late."

I had sensed Roni's growing impatience as the old man had rambled on.

"Yes," I said, "we must be getting home. It's very nearly dark."

And indeed, close as we stood to him, I had to strain through the gloom to see him as he hastily wrapped up my book in brown paper, which he tied into a parcel with string.

He escorted us down the shop between the booklined shelves which towered, cliff–like, on either side.

"Treasure the book," he said.

We walked past him into the tiny square, and I turned.

"I will. I can promise you that."

"Goodbye," said the old man.

He had not ventured over the threshold so that now, dark as it had become, he was scarcely visible and seemed, in a strange way, to be one with the shadows.

We left the courtyard by the short alley–way through which we had entered, and I remember distinctly that we turned left. Here, everything was brilliantly lit. Almost immediately we saw ahead a small coffee shop, its front piled high with Arab sweetmeats and pastries, their honey coating glistening under the bare electric bulbs.

I was determined to examine my latest acquisition under the lights, so we went in and ordered Turkish coffee and cakes. While waiting, I unwrapped my parcel. The book it contained was not in my hands for more than thirty seconds before I realised that old Monsieur Labac had made a terrible mistake.

I look up at Roni, aghast.

"He's given us the wrong volume. This isn't the reproduction – it's the original. He must have got confused. It was so dark in that shop. We must go back."

"Ruth, my darling," said Roni, "there's an old Latin saying that has governed the relations between buyers and sellers for thousands of years: *caveat emptor* – buyer beware. I think it holds true for sellers, too. And just think what that book could buy us – all the things we want."

"Nonsense," I said, "it couldn't buy us a family. And do you think I'm going to steal a book worth millions from that wonderful old man, simply because he made a natural human error. And especially after the way he treated me."

"You're right, of course," said Roni. "Come on, we'll go back. It's only round the corner."

We found the passageway without difficulty. When we re-emerged into the courtyard, the stillness was even more pronounced in contrast to the bustle we had just left, and the tiny shop in the far corner was silent and dark.

We went over, and I looked in vain for a bell or knocker. I rapped on the glass and called out "Monsieur Labac! Monsieur Labac!".

A tiny flicker of light glimmered far away in the recesses of the shop, like a remote star in the endless void of space. It advanced towards us, and at length I saw Monsieur Labac approaching, an oil lamp in his hand. He reached the front door and held the lamp high as he peered out.

"Who is it? What do you want? Mrs Illyon? Is that you?"

"Yes, Monsieur Labac," I called. "We had to come back."

The old man unlocked the door and pulled it open.

"It's the book you sold us," I said. "Take it. Look."

I thrust the volume into his hands. He put down the oil lamp and took it.

I don't know what reaction I had expected – horror, distress, amazement, relief. To me it seemed that his over–riding emotion was an immense satisfaction. He hugged the book to him.

"Mrs Illyon, Mrs Illyon. The original Book of the Cabal. You returned it to me, although I told you it was so valuable."

"It was the only thing to do."

"Ah, there you are mistaken," he said. "There are always choices, always decisions, always the chance to frustrate those who would foretell the shape of future events. Others rnight have decided differently – you and your husband chose to exercise your free will in this way. How can I ever thank you?"

I became a little embarrassed, remembering how Roni had been tempted.

"Think nothing of it," I said. "All I want is the book I bought from you."

"That of course you must have," he said, taking up the oil lamp and moving slowly off down the shop to the counter, where the other volume still lay. We followed, and eventually stood close to together in the gloom, the lamp casting a soft glow on our faces.

"Mr Illyon," he said, as he began wrapping the volume. "You remember what I was saying to you earlier? I might have predicted that you would return here with this infinitely precious volume; I could have tried to ordain it; but I could never have guaranteed it."

"I understand that," I said.

"Which is why I am diffident about what I have to say to you now, my dear Mrs Illyon. If it teaches us anything, the Cabal teaches that existence is not purposeless; on the contrary, each life is full of purpose – often frustrated, of course, because of that free will about which we have spoken. So when I say I foretell certain events, I do so because I can distinguish, however obliquely, certain purposes..."

I interrupted him.

"And if I were to ask you whether you were foretelling these events or pre–ordaining them...?"

"I would answer, perhaps, that the question is somewhat academic. And so I say to you, my dear Mrs Illyon, that before long you and your husband will find true fulfilment in your life together. Later you will travel abroad and become the recipient of a great fortune. This, dear Mrs Illyon, it is intended that you will use to wonderful effect to found a great library, here in this holy city of Jerusalem. This is the purpose, you are the chosen instrument. Because of it your name will be remembered for hundreds of years after you, and your husband, and I, have passed away from the earth. Listen, my dear Mrs Illyon, and remember..."

We left the shop, Roni and I, shaken as much by the intensity of the old man's vision as by his strange words. A week or so later, walking again through the old city, I tried to retrace my steps and find again the short alleyway and the tiny court, but all my efforts were in vain.

Thereafter, I made a point of scouring the old city from time to time, but never again did I set eyes upon that little courtyard with the bookshop in one corner.

So why has old Monsieur Labac been so much in my mind these last few days? The reason is quickly told.

For several years after our little adventure, Roni and I were too tied up with starting our small family and getting established in business to take a holiday abroad. Later, the truth is that we were scared – scared in case the old man's prophecy was not fulfilled, and scared in case it was: *You will travel abroad and become the recipient of a great fortune.* So we put off going time and again, giving each other excuse after excuse.

Eventually, the illness of a near and very dear member of our family forced us to put all reservations to one side and fly quickly to England. Fortunately our relative made a reasonable recovery, but while we were there Roni succumbed to the temptations of the English football pools. First dividends had topped two million in the week we arrived, and Roni couldn't resist. He filled in his pools coupon and posted it last Monday. On Tuesday we flew back to Israel. The games are to be played on Saturday. Think of us – picture our state of mind this weekend – as we sit glued to the radio listening to the English football scores on the BBC's World Service.

Monsieur Labac, where are you? I still have the book you sold me, so I know you existed. But who were you really? It was only yesterday, as I was idly writing your name again and again on a scrap of paper, that I realised just what your name spells – backwards.

\*

By mid-1990 Jerusalem was in the throes of a massive redevelopment aimed at beautifying and transforming a vast site below the walled old city. This description of what was afoot was published in the *Jewish Chronicle* in the issue of 5th of May 1990.

# OLD CITY – NEW FACE

Belying its age and the veneration lavished upon it, Jerusalem these days is exhibiting the go-ahead dynamism of a boom town. The scale and pace of civic and private sector development are astonishing in one of the world's major trouble spots, where all you might expect are insecurity, uncertainty, lack of confidence and a positive disinclination to invest.

This mushrooming of activity springs, of course, from the reuniting of the divided city in 1967 in the aftermath of the Six-Day War. Within days of the ending of hostilities, the Old City became the focus of intensive restoration and improvement. The sewage system was still based on the conduits built by the Turks up to 300 years before; 30 per cent of households had no electricity and two-thirds no running water.

A long-term project was put in hand and vigorously pursued, to install a modem drainage and sewage system and to renovate the water, electricity, telephone and television networks. Over the years, unsafe building foundations have been strengthened, façades repaired, and most of the Old City's streets repaved. All four quarters of the Old City bear witness to the effectiveness of the operation.

The Jewish Quarter, though, had been ravaged. The synagogues had been destroyed and many of the houses left in ruins. A plan not only to restore but to redevelop the area was devised, and because excavations had never before been carried out in the quarter, developers and archaeologists worked hand in hand.

As a result, the Jewish Quarter is today not only an intriguing area to visit, replete with alleys and courtyards and squares, but it preserves the major archaeological finds of the past twenty years such as the Roman market street known as the Cardo, and the Burnt House, a Vesuvius-like domestic record of the time the Second Temple was destroyed.

Jerusalem's new boundaries extended north as far as the Atarot Airport, taking in Neveh Ya'akov and Ramot, skirted Mount Scopus in the east – thus reincorporating the campus in the municipality – and swung round again well south of Ramat Rachel. Ever since, new housing projects, which one by one have blossomed into fully-fledged suburbs, have been a consistent feature of Jerusalem's development.

Ramat Eshkol, French Hill and Ma'alot Dafna were early suburbs, aimed primarily at linking Mount Scopus with the rest of the city. Subsequent neighbourhoods, constructed on the rocky hills that surround Jerusalem, now form a vast encircling city wall from Ramot in the north-west round to Gilo in the south.

Pisgat Ze'ev, the newest, links Neveh Ya'akov and French Hill, and is planned eventually to comprise 12,000 housing units. So far, 3,000 have been constructed. Now, word is that a new suburb to the south-east of the city is on the drawing-board; the rumoured location is Har Homa, south of the village of Tsur Bahir.

To provide for the expected wave of Russian aliyah over the next few years, the national plan is to produce 30,000 housing units as quickly as possible. Jerusalem's contribution is set at 5,000, and clearly the municipality will not be starting from scratch.

Smaller-scale developments to improve the appearance and facilities of Jerusalem are a continuous process, as any constant visitor to the city can testify.

Ten years ago, Ben Yehuda Street, a key thoroughfare in the centre of the city linking Jaffa Road with King George V Street, was a dangerous roadway with inadequate pavements, where vehicles and pedestrians were at perpetual loggerheads. Today, it is a sort of Israeli Carnaby Street, a pedestrian precinct dotted with open-air café tables. Buskers entertain, artists exhibit their work in the warm summer evenings, schoolchildren sell off unwanted books at the start of each term.

In fact, a recent municipal programme to rehabilitate "heart of town" districts is well under way. One notable example is the $10 million revitalisation of the Machane Yehudah market; other smaller projects are in varying stages of completion.

Major developments, though, require a long gestation period. One of the most important has its origins twenty years ago, in the aftermath of the 1967 reunification of the city.

Immediately outside the Old City walls, virtually facing the Jaffa Gate, lies the district of Mamilla. Strategically located at the geographic centre of the metropolis, it is not surprising that, when commerce began to develop in Jerusalem towards the end of the last century, Mamilla thrived. Shops, offices, warehouses, small factories, and eventually a hotel, gave Mamilla its unique character as the city's "new commercial centre."

The armistice lines of 1949, although encompassing Mamilla within Israeli Jerusalem, virtually killed off the area. Mamilla and Jaffa Streets were exposed to sniping by Jordanian soldiers from the Old City. To provide some protection, walls were erected down the middle of Mamilla Street, and the area rapidly deteriorated into a sort of no-man's-land.

In 1970, the Government and the municipality jointly gave the go-ahead to its redevelopment. A Central Jerusalem Development Company, known as Karta, was set up to start the long, complicated process of acquiring all the properties in the 28-acre central city site, evacuating and relocating the residents and businesses, and then razing the area to allow the development to proceed.

It was only in March 1989 that Britain's Ladbroke Group was awarded the contract to redevelop and rebuild Mamilla. Their plans, drawn up under the supervision of architect Moshe Safdie, comprise four main components: a commercial district, a boulevard and park, a residential quarter and a hotel area. A sign of the times is that every building contract will contain a clause obliging the contractors to employ Russian olim as specialists, technicians and construction personnel.

The site lies in a natural valley, and the new park and boulevard will occupy the valley floor, opening up vistas towards the Old City walls. The parkland will link the National Park around the Old City with Independence Park to the west, to form a great unbroken area of green in the heart of the city.

Mamilla Street, the main axis of the project, will be converted into a pedestrian shopping mall on two levels, while a retail arcade will link the mall to the Old City. The residential quarter will provide 200 units in five terrace rows of different heights, conforming to the natural topography of the site. Adjacent, along King David Street, lies the area designated for up to 550 new hotel rooms.

The $250 million project has not been without its critics – notably archaeological objections to the excavations just beyond the Jaffa Gate. Disputes have, however, been resolved, the work is progressing, and the two-level Mamilla mall could be open to the public early next year.

Multi-million dollar development projects are infectious. Consider the quite separate $80 million development just to the north of Mamilla which received official blessing only a few weeks ago. This, to be called City Hall Square, will concentrate all the municipal offices in one redeveloped area, a sort of municipal campus built around a large open plaza.

Then, halfway down the hill between the Hilton Hotel and the central bus station – betwixt heaven and hell, as it were – stands Jerusalem's convention centre, Binyanei Ha'uma. Work started some time ago on a $50 million project aimed at upgrading the facility into a congress centre equipped to top international standards.

Yet another vast enterprise is well under way down in the Manahat district, in the south-west of the city. Here an extraordinarily ambitious plan is afoot to create something in the nature of a city-wide community centre. An important component will inevitably be a shopping complex, to be provided by the highly successful Canadian entrepreneur, David Azriel, whose Israeli track record includes the flourishing centres at Ramat Gan and Beer-Sheva.

The most striking element, perhaps, is the much fought-over 12,000-seater sports stadium. Ultra-Orthodox objections, specifically to the idea of Shabbat football fixtures, have long perpetuated the bizarre situation of Jerusalem football teams home ground being sited in Tel Aviv. Now. construction of the stadium is forging ahead, not only for football, but as a general sports centre that will incorporate and expand the current Israel Tennis Centre. It should open its doors before the end of 1991.

The plans for Manahat extend well beyond these two projects, though. A hi-tech industrial park is envisaged, as part of broader public parklands which will also provide a new home for Jerusalem's famous Biblical Zoo. An arts school is planned; so is a new bus terminus and, if the recently established Jerusalem Development Corporation is to be believed, a new railway station as well. They are as yet, though, saying nothing about laying new track or providing new rolling stock (that currently in use dates back to British Mandate days).

Full marks, however, for taking on board a well-recognised principle of modern town planning – ensuring that the infrastructure is adequate to match the rest of the development. The principle is well in evidence when one looks at what is happening to Jerusalem's road system.

Anyone familiar with the drive from Ben Gurion airport to Jerusalem cannot fail to have noticed recent changes to the city's entrance. Branching off to the left, and curving up towards Ramot, a new road suddenly made its appearance in 1988. This will eventually be known as Highway 1.

Only last year, a second major road appeared, branching off to the right. To be dubbed Highway 4 when completed, this is planned to lead, via Givat Shaul and the Zion Valley, to the new shopping complex at Manahat.

I asked Teddy Kollek, Jerusalem's veteran mayor, which of the developments he regarded as the most significant for his city's future.

"I must admit that I am eager to see both City Hall Square and Mamilla completed," he said. "Both of these projects are located on the seam between East and West Jerusalem and will serve further to integrate the city."

Especially close to his heart is the sports stadium.

"I always saw it as the one promise I made to Jerusalemites that I did not fufil. When the first game is played there, I am sure I will experience a great sense of satisfaction."

*The Jewish Chronicle*
*18 May 1990*

\*

# THE PASSING SCENE – 5

Eventually, I am happy to report, the chaotic situation described here, was remedied, and Tel Aviv's new central bus station, a model of its kind, finally emerged in the late 1990's – ten years after this piece appeared in the *Jewish Telegraph*.

Look at any map of Tel Aviv published in the last 10 years, and down there in the south-western part of the city, you'll find a large area designated as the "New Bus Station". I would advise against trying to find it on the ground, because it doesn't exist. It represents a long-term aspiration – to the best of my knowledge, an aspiration years from realisation.

For the present, and the foreseeable future, anyone wishing to travel by bus to or from Tel Aviv must make use of the extraordinary "tachana ha'mercasit" – in other words, "Central Bus Station". I put the term in quotes because – as anyone who has ever visited it will testify – it is not so much a bus station as a bus district.

Oh, there *is* an open area where some buses line up in traditional style and passengers get on and off, but I would reckon that no more than half the buses that start or finish in Tel Aviv are accommodated there. The rest are located over an incredible number of adjoining streets, in most of which morning–to–night street markets are in raucous progress.

You pick your way through the accumulated debris, past barrow boys and stall–holders in full belt, seeking for the street where your particular bus is parked. And can you wander! It goes without saying that there is no published guide or direction indicator. In Israel you are expected to know these things – just as you are expected to know where the different "sheroots" (shared taxis) for Jerusalem or Haifa are located, with not a sign in view.

I bought a ticket for Zichron from the ticket office, and asked where the 871 or 872 left from. The clerk looked at me as if I were *meshuga* (mad) and waved vaguely behind him.

"*U'vul rechov mu?*" I asked ("But what street"?).

"*Lo yodai'u*" ("Don't know").

So that was that: I set off to scour the streets.

Yes, I located it in the end, and now I feel I know the Tel Aviv bus district very well indeed. But no one can keep that maze of streets and huge variety of bus routes in mind.

*

Start down the main road out of Jerusalem towards Tel Aviv, turn right just past the petrol station (you know the one!), and you're on the new Ramot road.

Opened within the past year, it winds northwards, a broad modern highway, up the Judean foothills to the suburb of Ramot. And just a couple of hundred yards along, a splendid new restaurant has just opened. Two or three abandoned dwellings have been cleverly adapted to provide a series of spacious eating areas, augmented by a couple of open–air balconies.

Sitting out here in the warm evening air, you gaze on a marvellous view across a broad valley out to the Judean hills beyond. Within, the decor is imaginative and full of surprises. I asked the "Maitre D" about it.

"The idea is to reflect both our Middle Eastern environment and our Western influences," he explained.

At strategic places in the dining areas, a wide variety of Arab artefacts and costumes are on display. While choosing from an extensive menu, which combines Israeli with international cuisine, you can puzzle over the exact use to which some of the objects would have been put.

And then the Western influences become apparent. A grandmother clock chimes out the quarters, Big Ben style: a genuine 1930s wind–up gramophone, complete with black 78 record, enlivens the entrance area, and in another nook a pre-war wireless set is on display.

*

Wandered into the Tel Aviv bookshop of the Society for the Preservation of Nature in Israel, a veritable treasure house of maps, publications and material of all kinds about the flora and fauna of Israel. And I learned the little known fact that the country, small as it is, boasts no less than 12 protected nature reserves. All are under the control of the Nature Reserves Authority, and between them they represent a full range of scenic beauty from the eagle observation point at Gamla in the Golan, to the coral reefs of Eilat in the Red Sea.

Among the other protected reserves are the swamp way-station at Hula, where multitudes of birds stop over on their Europe–Africa migration; the Avshalom stalactite and stalagmite caves; and Hai–Bar Yotvata, where biblical animals like the wildfox and the antelope are being systematically reintroduced into the land of Israel.

So I decided to make my own expedition to the Ein Gedi nature reserve. Hard by the Dead Sea Ein Gedi is virtually an oasis in the midst of the Judean desert. Waterfalls splash down into natural rock pools all the year round.

I plunged into one, clothed in tee–shirt and shorts, and was dry in five minutes. In the lush, hilly, well–watered area ibexes, hyraxes and leopards flourish. Quite a day's outing!

*

Which led me, some fifteen years later, to write this letter to the Daily Telegraph. A poll of people's view of other countries had placed Israel at the bottom of the world's list in virtually every category, including "beauty". This response appeared on the 12th of January 2005.

The Editor
Daily Telegraph

Sir

As someone who travels to Israel regularly, I am saddened by the lack of knowledge of the country. That it tops the list of "least beautiful countries" is due to a misconception. The range of environments contained within this small country is amazing. Travelling from the ski resort of Mount Hermon in the north, to the undersea wonders of Eilat in the far south, you encompass such phenomena as the Dead

Sea and the awe–inspiring silence of the Negev desert. This is to say nothing of the biblical locations.

Israel is a vibrant, multi–cultural and fully democratic nation deserving of a far better opinion than we currently seem prepared to afford it.

Yours, etc

\*

Fully democratic, indeed, and as such continually riven by internal political and cultural dissension. Take, for example, the sudden resignation of David Levy, in April 1992, from Benjamin Netanyahu's cabinet.

# MONKEY PUZZLE

*London*

When news of David Levy's threatened resignation broke in London, news commentators tried to get to grips with the underlying causes of the spat. A well–known BBC journalist on the early morning radio news show "Today" interviewed a Levy spokesman from Jerusalem. During the interchange he tried to make sense of Levy's complaint about being treated liked a monkey just down from the trees.

"Is there," he wanted to know, "some underlying racial split in Israeli society that the world hears little about?"

The spokesman prevaricated and turned the question aside, but the fact that it could be asked by one of the BBC's leading domestic broadcasters shows how little is known about the Ashkenaz/Sephardi divide outside Jewish circles.

I suppose the general feeling in the diaspora is that the children of the first Magic Carpet influx of the early–1950s must by now have become more or less fully integrated into "sabra society". We understand, though, (none better) that more time needs to elapse before the later waves of immigrants from the Sephardi world – to say nothing of the Falashas – can be as completely absorbed.

But then, we realise, the complexities of the divide are being exacerbated by the inflow of new Ashkenazi immigrants from Russia and the other east European countries. In a sense the old 1948 balance is being restored – but only as regards the proportionate strengths of the two elements.

Everything else has changed. Today the Sephardis have a self-confidence they certainly lacked in the old days, and at least one major national figurehead through whom to express their individual political approach. The newest unabsorbed immigrants, on the other hand, are the latest Ashkenazi influx.

We understand that it would be simplistic to assert that these two major sectors in Israeli society are divided simply by different religious traditions. As simplistic, we in the UK can appreciate, as asserting that the so–called Catholic–Protestant divide in Northern Ireland is essentially a religious one. The fault–line in society runs deep – that we can accept. As in Northern Ireland, it encompasses economic, educational and social factors expressed through the jejune language of religious difference. What does puzzle some of us, though, is the way this particular politico–religious cookie has crumbled.

The accepted wisdom out here in the diaspora has been that the Sephardis were the hawks of Israeli society. They, or their parents, had been born or bred in the heart of the Arab world. Intimate experience of living among and dealing with Arabs had enabled them to understand the Arab mentality in a way no effete Westerner ever could. This explained their consistent support for the tough approach ("strength is the only message the Arab understands"). We believed that Begin was originally swept to power on a wave of support from Sephardi Jews, blossoming for the first time into full political awareness. Hard–line Likud policy has, we understood, rested ever since on the rock–steady girder of Sephardi solidarity with the hawks of the right.

These preconceptions seem to have been overturned by the latest play of events. What are we to make of the news that the Israeli Foreign Minister is about to leave the Government because it rejects his conciliatory policies towards the peace process? Has the leading representative of the Sephardi hawks been misreported? And if not, can he actually be speaking for the Sephardi constituency from which he has sprung? A certain credence seems to attach to this latter possibility by the stories (rumours?) that Levy is intent on establishing a breakaway political party and taking his Sephardi supporters with him.

And then those of us with longer memories recall Moshe Dayan, in his time perhaps the politician most knowledgeable about Arab society. He was tough enough, in all conscience, when occasion demanded. Yet his understanding of the Arab world, far from leading him towards confrontation, drew him consistently in the direction of conciliation. Is there, then, some bizarre parallel to be drawn between Dayan and Levy? Do left–wing Ashkenazi and right-wing Sephardi actually meet on the remote side of the political sphere?

So many preconceptions about the way the world wags have been overturned in the past couple of years that nowadays anything has begun to seem feasible.

*

In the mid-1990s, I visited Masada yet again.

# RETURN TO MASADA

Last Chanukah I went back to Masada. If "Chanukah" spells the miraculous start of the Maccabean kingdom, "Masada" spells its inspiring end. Masada is one of those places in Israel you feel compelled to return to from time to time.

However many times you may have seen it, you are struck anew with its stark and overwhelming beauty. It exercises its powerful influence whatever the season or time of day, and however many tourists may have decided to choose to visit at the same time.

Masada is essentially a great rocky outcrop rising sheer and stark out of the desert landscape that leads down to the Dead Sea. There are other, similar rocky places in the area, but what distinguishes Masada is first its sheer size, and secondly its peculiar flat top – almost as if some giant had taken a carving knife and sliced it. In itself, then, Masada would be a natural phenomenon well worth a visit, rather like Ayers Rock in the centre of Australia. What attracts its unending stream of tourists, however, is the central role that Masada played in the struggle for Jewish independence against the Romans two thousand years ago.

For Masada was the last redoubt of the tiny remnant of the Maccabees – the Jewish freedom fighters who held out against the might of Rome even when all hope of victory had been long extinguished. Up to that virtually impregnable natural fortress they retreated, with their wives and children. And up there, in a settlement which included homes, storehouses, a synagogue, a mikva – all still on view – they held out for three years while far below, camped out on the desert sands, the Roman legions beseiged and continually harried them.

The story is well known of how the Roman Governor, Flavius Silva, finally devised a method of scaling the heights, and of how, in a final act of defiance, the entire Jewish community of nearly a thousand souls, led by Eleazar ben Yair, committed an act of mass suicide rather than fall into the enemy's hands.

"And so," writes the Jewish chronicler, Josephus, who actually lived through these events, "the Romans were met with piles of dead bodies. But they gained no satisfaction from the sight, even though it was their enemies who lay dead. All they could do was marvel at the courage of their decision, and at the unshakeable contempt for death which hundreds of individuals had shown in carrying it through."

Go up to the flat top of Masada by way of the cable car, and stand on the ramparts. There, far below to the north–west and south–east you can still see, preserved it seems forever in the sands, the outlines of the Roman camps – the walls, the roadways, the earthworks. This is where, for three years, thousands of Roman soldiers, auxiliaries and prisoners of war lived and worked, constructing the great scaling ramp that was eventually to lead to the fall of the last Jewish stronghold.

As you stand high above the desert, the Dead Sea visible on the horizon, you can almost imagine you can hear the trumpets and bugle calls from the military camps far below – just as those defiant but doomed Jewish defenders of Masada must have grown accustomed to, during the long months of their seige.

One of the first questions that springs to mind when you visit Masada is: how did a beseiged community in the middle of the desert, entirely cut off from help, manage for water?

The answer is one of the most fascinating aspects of the place. Half a century before the Jewish defenders captured it, part of Masada had been converted into an extraordinary rural palace by Herod. Much of the palace has been excavated and is now open to the visitor. It is an amazing sight. Constructed up the sheer north face of the rock, it exists on three separate levels. The views out over the desert are quite spectacular, and the living areas, bathhouses, gardens, swimming pool, terraces, are the height of Roman luxury.

A mind–boggling feature are the vast interior water storage chambers, constructed so as to be replenished from water flows that are fed by the autumn and winter rains. In this part of the desert great wadis run down from the interior to the Dead Sea. For many months they are bone dry, and seem to be simply great gouges scored across the sandstone. But at certain times, and terrifyingly fast, flash flooding can turn them into raging torrents. Almost every year, it seems, the papers report that some hapless driver has been swept off the road that skirts the Dead Sea by an unexpected and massive flow of water down one of the wadis.

It was this water flow that the Roman engineers tapped and ingeniously diverted into great reservoirs that they hewed out of the rocky interior of Masada itself. The amount trapped during the brief rainy season was so great that it was more than sufficient to maintain an extensive royal court and military garrison during Herod's time, and the beseiged Jewish defenders and their families later on.

Indeed, as far as water went during the seige, the Jews were consistently better off than the Romans toiling away in the baking sands, where every drop was precious and had to be carted from the nearest oasis.

To experience a sense of involvement with events long past but still vivid, there are few places you can visit that surpass Masada. At Chanukah time in particular a visit to Masada sets the story of the Maccabees into a timeless context. The Jewish state that they fought for, won and lost is, after two thousand years, again a reality.

\*

# THE PASSING SCENE – 6

Situated on high ground in Jerusalem's exclusive Talbiyeh area, hard by the President's official residence and the major foreign Embassies, the Jerusalem Theatre stands, as a symbol of the capital's commitment to the arts. It is a beautiful building from the outside, and magnificent within. Broad corridors and staircases carpeted in red serve to link theatres and halls of various sizes. The largest is often used for concerts by the Israel Philharmonic as well as by other Israeli and visiting orchestras. Smaller halls house theatrical and film performances and other musical events. There are bars and restaurants, and the complex is also used for exhibitions or various sorts.

I was intrigued to hear of an exhibition of photographs taken recently in Poland. 1 had no idea what to expect, but I found the visit very rewarding.

In 1939 Poland's Jewish population totalled 3½ million. Today there are less than 5,000 in the country. Tomasz Tomaszewski set out to make a photographic record of these surviving vestiges of what was once a large and thriving community. He took 7,000 pictures in all.

From a selection he created a book, "Remnants", which won the underground Solidarity award for the best cultural achievement in 1985. The Jerusalem Theatre recreated his book in exhibition form.

And there they were – *haimishe* Jewish faces, rich and poor, young and old, men and women, struggling to keep alive a token of the religion and way of life in clearly appallingly unfavourable circumstances.

An apology of a Chanukah party in an upstairs church hall with pitifully few children; an aged Hebrew teacher with a "Talmud Torah" of one. Aged men and women live alone in shabby surroundings clinging to their memories. Someone discovers a desecrated tombstone inscribed in Hebrew under the floor of a barn.

Yet, of course, there is still laughter. A few actors actually maintain a sketchy Yiddish theatre for the community.

If one legacy of Hitler's Final Solution is today's State of Israel, another is to be found in the lives of the tiny Jewish community in Poland.

*

I flew into Ben Gurion from Athens, travelling El Al, and was greatly surprised by the first announcement over the intercom. In accordance with Israel's recent law, we were informed, the flight was entirely non–smoking,

I asked a delightful air hostess, Miriam, about the new arrangements.

"El Al is following the American and British airlines," she explained. "We're all making domestic and short–haul flights completely smoke-free. The flight time from Athens to Tel Aviv is only about 90 minutes, and we think people can do without a cigarette that long. It makes for a much better working atmosphere, I can tell you."

The new deal is certainly a great relief to us non-smokers. No matter how far into the non-smoking area you go, the smell of cigarettes always penetrates.

Of course, smoking has been banned on the buses in Israel for a couple of years, and now restrictions on smoking are being extended to cover a range of other public places. Only a few years ago veryone in Israel seemed to smoke like chimneys–it was even a penance to enter most banks and post offices, to say nothing of the cinemas.

Now all that's changing – and very much for the better.

\*

Tel Aviv seems to have entered on a building boom – or rather a re–building boom. Visiting the city after some time, I was surprised at the amount of reconstruction being undertaken in the old town area. Many of the early, now very run–down, buildings on the original site of the city are being swept away and being replaced by impressive modern creations,

The story is well known of how a group of Zionist pioneers in 1908 plodded along the sea shore north of the port of Jaffa. After a mile or so they stopped in the midst of unbroken sand stretching on three sides and said: "This is where we will build the first all–Jewish city."

The name first used for what was, in effect, a Jewish residential neighbourhood within the Jaffa municipality, was Ahuzat Bayit. Two years later, in 1910, it adopted as its name the title chosen for the Hebrew translation of Herzl's Zionist vision: "Altneuland".

In the original German, Herzl's book title meant "Old new–land". The Hebrew translator, Nahum Sokolow, used the word "tel" (meaning old ruin) for the first part. and "aviv" (meaning spring, or renewal) for the second.

The old town, with its pre–World War 1 buildings, tended to spread away from Jaffa up towards the north. So the further up the coast one went, the more modern the buildings. Some time within the last ten years the process has been reversed, and the Tel Aviv seafront has been creeping south, closer and closer to Jaffa itself, which retains its strong Arab character.

The run–down and decrepit buildings of old Tel Aviv – most of them with little architectural merit – became something of an eyesore sandwiched between the more substantial parts of the city. Now the renewal process is in full flood, part of the beautification of the city, being spearheaded by the popular mayor, Shlomo ("Chich") Lahat. It is clear that Tel Aviv is making a bid to become one of the most desirable beach resorts in the world.

*

To mark the 50th anniversary of the State of Israel, I put to BBC Radio 3 the idea of two 120-minute programmes tracing the story of the Israel Philharmonic Orchestra and the relationship between the orchestra's history and that of the State. Although the orchestra was founded in 1936 as the Palestine Orchestra by the outstanding Jewish-Polish violinist, Bronislaw Huberman, the Israel Philharmonic Orchestra *as such* dates its birth from the same moment as that of the State, the 14th of May 1948. Composed of European musicians fleeing from Nazism, the Palestine Orchestra gave its first concert on the 26th of December 1936 under the baton of Arturo Toscanini.

The two programmes were broadcast on BBC Radio 3 on Friday the 8th and Friday the 15th of May 1998. The narrator was Sheena McDonald, and the programmes included contributions from Leonard Bernstein and Arthur Rubinstein, and interviews with Zubin Mehta, Kurt Masur, Isaac Stern, Daniel Barenboim, Pinchas Zukerman, Yitzhak Perlman, Noam Sheriff and some half-dozen current members of the orchestra.

Thanks to the invaluable assistance of the head of English programmes for Kol Yisrael, Sara Manobla, the musical content contained a wealth of recorded music from the archives of Kol Yisrael that had never been heard before in this country, among them:

Schoenburg's "A Survivor from Warsaw" narrated and sung in Hebrew recorded in 1962 in Jerusalem;

The only recording of Serge Koussevistsky with the IPO, playing Mozart's Divertimento No 15, recorded in October 1950;

The world première of Noam Sheriff's "Festival Prelude" conducted by Leonard Bernstein at the inauguration concert at the Mann Auditorium in October 1957;

Artur Rubinstein playing Brahms Piano Concerto No 1 at his last concert with the IPO at the age of 89, recorded in April 1976;

The "Ode to Joy" from Beethoven's 9th Symphony sung in Hebrew, conducted by Rafael Kubelik and recorded in April 1958;

Stravinsky conducting the IPO in a performance of his own Firebird Suite, recorded in Jerusalem in September 1962;

And a performance of Beethoven's 5<sup>th</sup> Symphony, conducted by Zubin Mehta, and played by the combined forces of the Israel Philharmonic and the Berlin Philharmonic – a unique 160-piece orchestra assembled for one night only in 1990, the Israel Philharmonic dressed in white and the Berlin Philharmonic in black..

In addition, the programmes included sound archive recordings made at the declaration of the State of Israel on 14 May 1948, at the victory concert on Mount Scopus after the 6-Day War, and the near-riot at Zubin Mehta's attempt to have the IPO play the music of Richard Wagner in 1981.

*

# THE ORCHESTRA AND THE PEOPLE
## The story of the Israel Philharmonic

Friday the 14<sup>th</sup> of May, 1948. As the final hours of the British mandate in Palestine tick away, David Ben Gurion gives orders for the ceremony to mark the birth of the Jewish State. The mandate is to expire at midnight. Ben Gurion decides to make the historic declaration just before shabbat comes in.

In the fevered atmosphere of the time, his over–riding concern is security. If the location becomes public knowledge, a single terrorist bomb could wipe out the entire embryonic government of the new State, together with most of its notables. So it is not till the middle of that Friday morning that officials begin telephoning the 200 people who have been selected to attend the ceremony. Only then are they told that it is to take place in Tel Aviv's Municipal Museum on Rothschild Boulevard at exactly 4 pm.

A further 50 or so people also received a call that morning, instructing them to be present – the members of what was then the Palestine Philharmonic Orchestra. For by 1948 the national orchestra had become so 'identified with the Jewish people that an occasion of such historic significance would have been unthinkable without their presence.

As the National Council and the guests made their way to the ground floor area, the orchestra assembled in the museum's upper gallery. At exactly 4 pm David Ben Gurion rapped the table with his gavel. This was the pre–arranged signal for the orchestra to strike up "Hatikvah". Unfortunately someone missed his cue, and from up aloft there came only silence. Never one to lack initiative, Ben Gurion promptly launched his uncertain voice into the anthem; rather raggedly the other members of the People's Council joined in.

After proclaiming the new State, Ben Gurion invited the members of the People's Council, one by one, to sign the document. As the last, Moshe Shertok, put his name to the scroll to thunderous applause, the orchestra finally made its presence known, and brought the proceedings to a close with "Hatikvah".

When the musicians assembled at the Municipal Museum that Friday afternoon, they did so as the Palestine Philharmonic Orchestra. By the time they played "Hatikvah" they had become the Israel Philharmonic Orchestra – the title they have borne ever since.

Give or take a few months, the orchestra was already twelve years old.

In the early 1930s the increasingly harsh race laws being imposed in Germany roused the eminent Polish–Jewish violinist, Bronislaw Huberman, to a fury. In newspaper letters and articles he roundly berated German intellectuals for failing to stand up for freedom of cultural expression, and he tried to mobilise world opinion against the persecution of Jewish writers, artists and musicians inside Germany.

Finally, he decided to do something practical to help those of his own profession who were being denied the right to perform inside the Third Reich. He began to persuade first–rank Jewish musicians to emigrate to Palestine. Against all the odds, he succeeded in setting up a viable orchestra largely made up of immigrant musicians. Even more remarkably, he managed to persuade perhaps the most eminent conductor in the world at that time – Arturo Toscanini – to conduct the opening concert of the nascent orchestra on the 26th of December 1936.

"I am doing this for humanity," the maestro declared.

The first years were not easy. Not only had the 75 players brought a wide diversity of styles with them, but the diversity of languages added a further difficulty. Despite the problems, though, they quickly coalesced into an orchestra that eminent conductors were happy to lead, among others Molinari, Steinberg, Dobrowan and even Dr Malcolm Sargent, as he then was (the version of "Hatikvah" currently used by the orchestra is based on the setting made by Sargent in those early days).

If it was recognised remarkably early as a first–class orchestra, the Israel Philharmonic is now, by common consent, world class. The transformation has been due to two towering figures in its history – Leonard Bernstein and Zubin Mehta. Though one was a Jew and the other is not, they share equal credit for forging the unique symbiosis between the orchestra and the people of Israel that is the outstanding characteristic of the IPO.

No other top flight orchestra in the world is so closely identified with its constituency as the Israel Philharmonic. City orchestras in the States, the UK, Europe; national orchestras in the Netherlands, Switzerland and elsewhere – none are woven, as the IPO is, into the very fabric of their audience's lives. Where the Israeli people have gone, there has been the orchestra, giving musical expression to the great events in the nation's story.

Bernstein arrived in Israel in October 1948 to open the first orchestral season in the State of Israel. The season included six special concerts for service men and women – the most spectacular in the town of Beer–Sheva just captured from Egyptian troops. Braving bad roads, sand and dust, the orchestra travelled from Tel Aviv with their own piano, and played their concert on a makeshift stage before a thousand–strong audience of troops.

That November Bernstein broadcast from Israel to the States.

"Last week," he said, "we gave a concert in Jerusalem for soldiers only. Imagine 2,000 soldiers simultaneously given leave one morning in a city under siege! Imagine them crowding into the Edison Theatre, filling every nook, suspended literally from the roof, curled up on window–sashes, packed into the aisles and staircases – all to hear a Brahms symphony. And at the end, the shouting and screaming was an almost unbearable tribute. Yes, the orchestra is the lifeblood of Israel culture, and I am dedicated to the task of seeing it flourish."

A commitment he honoured to the full in the years that followed.

"From the first moment Bernstein stood before the orchestra," says Dr Uri Toeplitz, original flautist in the Palestine Orchestra and now the IPO's historian, "the relationship was instantaneous. We realised what a genius we had in front of us. Every concert with Bernstein was extraordinary."

Towards the end of May 1967, with Israel's Arab neighbours mobilising on her borders, the eminent conductor engaged for the summer concert series took fright and hurriedly departed. In the middle of the six days of fighting that began on the 5th of June, Zubin Mehta arrived from Europe in a plane otherwise filled with ammunition, joining Daniel Barenboim and Jacqueline du Pré who were already performing with the orchestra. Close on their heels came Sir John Barbirolli and Leonard Bernstein.

In July 1967, with Jerusalem once again united, an unforgettable concert was staged in the amphitheatre on Mount Scopus. In the warm summer afternoon, before a packed audience that included the President, the Prime Minister and David Ben Gurion, Bernstein conducted a performance of Mahler's 'Resurrection' symphony that lives in the memory of those present as an almost unbearably moving experience.

By this time Zubin Mehta's connection with the Israel Philharmonic, that has lasted to this day, was already strong, forged in his first season with the orchestra in 1961.

"When I came on to the stage for the second rehearsal," he recalls, "the players applauded."

How an Indian, coming to this group of Jewish musicians assembled from around the world, managed to create so extraordinary and lasting a chemistry, is something of a mystery. Mehta himself sometimes ascribes it to the fact that, as a Parsi, he himself is a member of a minority in his own country – though, he adds, the Parsis have never experienced racism like the Jews.

In the heady days that followed the Six Day War – days that saw the marriage of Barenboim and Jacqueline du Pré in Jerusalem – Mehta alternated with Bernstein in conducting the IPO in a series of victory concerts. The opening of the 1968/69 season coincided with the announcement of Mehta's appointment as musical director, an appointment extended for life in 1981.

"I will stay for as long as the players want me," declared maestro Mehta, in accepting the honour.

In the interim, during the Yom Kippur war in 1973, the orchestra under Mehta had toured ceaselessly inside Israel, playing before Israel Defense Force audiences from the Golan Heights to Sinai. During the Gulf War, Mehta cancelled his commitments and flew to Israel to conduct the IPO amid the Scud missile attacks.

It is under Mehta that the Israel Philharmonic has finally achieved acknowledged world class status. He has melded the rich string sound that comes so naturally to European musicians with the special qualities of brass and woodwind that flourish in the United States. He has provided the inspired leadership that unites a body of musicians into a musical instrument that is greater than its parts. Above all, he has cherished and fostered the unique relationship that has existed from the first between the orchestra and the people of Israel. Under his baton the IPO has been transformed into the musical expression of the nation's very identity.

\*

# DISGUSTED OF TUNBRIDGE WELLS

Finally, a few more missives fired off at one or other newspaper over the years which succeeded in hitting the mark – of publication, that is, not of affecting the issue in question to any noticeable extent. But the final letter, of February 2008, remains my fervent hope and dream.

\*

The Editor
The Jewish Chronicle

Sir,

George Bernard Shaw, in "Pygmalion", makes the point that as soon as an Englishman speaks, he makes some other Englishman despise him. British people have an acute awareness of accent, and credibility often stands or falls on how people express themselves. It is surely not beyond the wit of the Israeli government to recognise this.

*27 July 2002*

\*

The Editor
The Times

Sir,

Mr Paul Oddie (letter, August 2) places himself "in the middle ground", having implicitly laid the responsibility for 55 years of conflict at Israel's door, from the day in 1947 when the UN voted for a two–state solution for what was then Palestine.

Israel occupies the West Bank and Gaza because the territories were overrun during a war. Since that time Egypt has renounced sovereignty over Gaza, and Jordan over the West Bank. Only a political agreement, involving the establishment of a Palestinian sovereign state, can resolve the situation, but as long as there are terrorist groups like Hamas set on frustrating any such effort, how can a settlement be achieved?

*3 August 2002*

\*

The Editor,
The Jewish Chronicle.

Sir,

I am genuinely sorry that so cultivated a man as Gerald Kaufman can allow himself to be so blinkered about his own people and about Israel as he showed in his TV documentary, "End of the Affair."

In the context of the 5,000–year-old covenant between the Almighty and the Jewish people, does one transient Prime Minister merit the degree of loathing that Mr Kaufman heaps on Ariel Sharon?

Just as Sharon was democratically elected into office, he will assuredly be voted out again. If Mr Kaufman and like–minded Israelis find the present government's handling of the conflict unacceptable, the solution surely is to win over hearts and minds for an alternative strategy. However, since he has washed his hands of Israel, this is not an approach that Mr Kaufman seems to espouse.

Broaden your horizons Mr Kaufman. Basically, Israel is a wonderful, vibrant country, and the Jewish people springs from a tradition that provides the foundation for Western concepts of morality and justice. A way will be found.

*20 September 2002*

\*

The Editor
The Independent

Sir,

Robin Cook (Opinion, 10 October) seems to believe that a referendum of the Palestinian people on the two–state solution to the Middle East conflict would result in "a strong mandate" for the Palestinian leadership to pursue the road–map. Is it not just as likely that the result of the constant outpouring of anti–Israel, anti–Jewish propaganda in the Arab media might result in a different outcome? The two–state solution is no part of the agenda of Hamas, Islamic Jihad and the other terrorist organisations. Their openly acknowledged aim is the abolition of the state of Israel. The concept of a Jewish homeland in the historic land of Palestine – endorsed by the Balfour declaration, the League of Nations and the United Nations – is anathema to them. The real question is how far their influence has already rendered a peaceful solution to the conflict beyond reach. In an article that does not once mention Yasser Arafat – a malign influence on the road–map process if ever there was one – Robin Cook is chasing chimeras.

*11 October 2003*

*

The Editor,
The Independent

Sir,

Anne Penketh quotes one of the ex–diplomat authors of the letter to Tony Blair as saying: "All of us who signed the letter had been concerned over the last year or so that Middle Eastern expertise in the Foreign Office had been ignored by No 10" (Backlash begins against 'camel corps' plotters", 28 April).

The charge was that Tony Blair had abandoned the principles that have guided international efforts to restore peace in the Holy Land for forty years. Forty years, let us remind ourselves, of total failure, despite the Foreign Office's "Middle Eastern expertise". Every peace plan brokered by the international community has floundered. From Oslo to the Road Map, the pusillanimity of the Palestinian leadership in the face of the extremists within their ranks has destroyed every chance for peace.

The time for new – even lateral – thinking was long overdue. Full credit to Bush and Blair for recognising that if the Palestinians will not themselves take the necessary action to establish their sovereign state, then perhaps it should be thrust upon them. With Gaza evacuated by the Israelis and handed over, the terrorists will for once have been out–manoeuvred. This is one move towards a two–state solution they cannot scupper. Negotiations on Oslo/Road Map lines might then stand a chance.

*29 April 2004*

*

The Editor
The Times

Sir,

For some years Israel has been forced to play its "home" soccer games at various European venues because of fears about the unique security threat posed by potential terrorist attacks. When Tel Aviv was nominated as the venue for the European basketball finals, the organising body was planning to look elsewhere. However, representations from within Israel led the organisers to review the terrorist threat worldwide. The result convinced them that Israel posed no more of a security risk than any other European location, while the quality of Israel's security services was as high as that to be found anywhere in Europe. As a result, the final of the European basket-ball championships was played last weekend in Tel Aviv.

This seems a prime example of denying terrorists the victory of disrupting the life of ordinary citizens. Uefa has now lifted its boycott, and I hope that other bodies controlling international sport will follow suit.

*6 May 2004*

*

The Editor
The Jewish Chronicle

Sir,

Dr Tony Klug (Letters, September 1) is surely on the right lines. Despite, or perhaps because of, Tony Blair's recent efforts to provide some sort of balance to public perceptions about Israel's situation, lack of understanding and misinformation about Israel seems to grow relentlessly.

I was initially opposed to the idea of a publicity campaign in this country in support of Israel. My view has changed. I now believe that a series of statements in the press and on billboards might help redress the balance, and bring a better atmosphere to the debate.

The messages are not complicated.

The people of Israel want, above all, to live at peace with their neighbours.

Israel wants to end the Palestinian conflict through the establishment of a Palestinian state alongside Israel. But the present Palestinian government, which declares that it seeks to destroy Israel utterly, can scarcely be a partner for such negotiations. This dilemma must be resolved before the problem can be solved.

Israel has no argument with the Lebanese people. But the Lebanese government permitted a terrorist organisation to take control of part of its territory adjacent to Israel, amass a vast cache of weaponry, and rain rockets down on Israel. As soon as this danger has been satisfactorily sorted out, Israel will withdraw its troops to within its own boundaries.

Israel looks forward to a time when all the states in the region can live in peaceful co-operation with each other – when Israel, Jordan, Palestine and Lebanon might come together, on the lines of the Benelux countries, to form an economic grouping that could bring unparalleled prosperity to the Middle East.

*8 September 2006*

\*

To mark the 40<sup>th</sup> anniversary of the 6-Day War, *The Guardian*
invited the Prime Ministers of Israel and of the Palestinian
Authority to contribute statements of their respective
positions. The pieces, by Ehud Olmert and Ismail Haniyeh
respectively, appeared in the issue of June 6<sup>th</sup>, 2007. Struck
by the contrast between the tone of the two contributions, I
wrote to *The Guardian*. My letter appeared on the 8<sup>th</sup> of June.

The Editor
The Guardian

Sir,

Compare the two prime ministerial statements. From Olmert, a
reasoned case for compromise and peace based on the two-state solution that has now gained wide acceptance in the region and beyond.
From Haniyeh a diatribe without a hint of compromise, and a reit-
eration of demands that would effectively end Israel's existence as a
sovereign Jewish state.

Haniyeh's statement exemplifies the current insolubility of the
conflict.

The essential pre-requisite for Israel relinquishing its occupation
is the establishment of a sovereign Palestinian state to whom the territories can be handed over; at the moment neither Gaza nor the West
Bank belong to any sovereign nation. That cannot come about until
Israelis are able to sit down with partners prepared to negotiate a
settlement.. While Hamas continues to call and to work for Israel's
destruction, the essential first step to a solution of the problem will
continue to elude us.

*8 June 2007*

\*

The Editor
The Daily Telegraph

Sir

As Con Coughlin points out (June 15) Israel is now encircled by a Hamàs-dominated south and a Hizbollah-dominated north, both armed and supported by Iran to the east – all three determined on Israel's destruction.

Unsettling though this must be for Israel, the growing dominance of Islamic fundamentalism has much wider implications.

Despite Left-wing opinion to the contrary, the Israel-Palestine situation is not the motivation of fundamentalist action. Israel's destruction is a by-product of much wider objectives, which are well-publicised, but of which world opinion has seen fit to take little account, as yet.

Yours, etc.

*16 June 2007*

\*

Towards the end of 2007 talk of substantive peace negotiations again surfaced. Tony Blair, released from the burdens of office as UK Prime Minister, was engaged in intensive efforts to enhance the peace process, restrained – so the word went – by US Secretary of State Condoleeza Rice from taking too open an initiative. She, however, proposed heading a meeting in November 2007 in the USA east coast city of Annapolis, attended by Israeli Prime Minister Ehud Olmert and Palestinian Authority President Mahmoud Abbas, which, it was hoped, would lead to substantive peace negotiations. In this newly febrile atmosphere, the perennial issue of the future of Jerusalem again broke surface in the columns of the Jewish Chronicle, which reported that plans were well advanced in PM Olmert's office for dividing the city between Israel and a newly-sovereign Palestinian state. Vehement opposition to living with a "divided Jerusalem" was already being voiced. I wrote to the Jewish Chronicle to point out that everything depended on how you define "Jerusalem". My letter appeared in the issue of 16 November 2007.

The Editor
The Jewish Chronicle

Sir

A solution acceptable to all parties depends on how you define Jerusalem.

The municipal boundaries of Jerusalem, which Israel lived with from 1948 to 1967, were radically redrawn after the 6-Day War, and have been subject to a number of revisions since. The obvious solution is to redefine the boundaries of Jerusalem one last time – and, in so doing, to define the boundaries of a new municipality, Al-Quds. The new Jerusalem municipality would encompass the Jewish suburbs and as many of the settlements in the current Jerusalem as practicable; the municipality of Al-Quds, the mainly Arab suburbs, and also the adjacent Arab towns of the West Bank.

An agreed redrawing of boundaries would enable Israel to have Jerusalem as its undivided capital, while the new sovereign Palestinian state would acquire its own sister capital, Al-Quds. This solution would, of course, still leave the matter of the administration of the holy places in the Old City for resolution.

*16 November 2007*

\*

The Editor
The Jerusalem Report

The strand of Palestinian strategic thinking that Ehud Ya'ari discerns (Jan. 21) has a certain rationality behind it. A newly-created sovereign Palestinian state sitting alongside Israel would indeed struggle to reach viability, let alone prosperity. However, to abandon the two-state solution is not the only, or indeed a preferable, way out of the difficulty – certainly not from the point of view of Israel as a Jewish homeland. For example, with a sovereign Palestine up and running, the way is open for a new configuration in the region – a formal confederation of Israel, Palestine, Jordan and Lebanon on the lines of the Benelux countries within the European Union. An economic alliance along these lines could open the way to dynamic growth and development in the region on a previously unimaginable scale. Perhaps Palestinian opinion would embrace this model of "independence with cooperation" with equal enthusiasm, if it were on offer.

*18 February 2008*

*

# THE SERPENT'S SMILE

Olga Hesky was born in London and went to South Africa in 1940. In 1949 she emigrated to Israel, married an Israeli government official, and edited a woman's magazine for ten years. In 1966 she published her first thriller with an up-to-date Israeli setting – *The Serpent's Smile*. She followed this up with three others, before her death in 1974.

In 1984 I put to BBC Radio 4 the idea of a dramatisation of *The Serpent's Smile* for the popular radio drama slot, Saturday Night Theatre. At that time there had been virtually no drama on BBC radio set in Israel, and the proposal was taken up. The producer was John Cardy, a friend and working colleague as editor of "A Book at Bedtime".

*The Serpent's Smile* was, of course, published a year before the Six Day War, but we agreed to set the play in contemporary Israel. By that time I'd come to know the head of radio drama for Kol Yisrael, Eran Baniel, and we contacted him and asked if he would help our production by recording some genuine Israeli sound effects: Tel Aviv traffic, Israeli telephone tones and police sirens... things like that. After a time the sound effect tapes arrived, and John Cardy fed them as appropriate into the production.

The play was broadcast on Radio 4 on the night of Saturday the 16th of February 1985, and was repeated the following Monday afternoon. The part of Tami was played by Steve Hodson, Shelley by Susan Deneker and Papa Barzilai by John Gabriel. Also in the cast were two well-known Jewish actors of the time – Cyril Shaps and Harry Towb.

*The Serpent's Smile....*

\*

# THE SERPENT'S SMILE

*A play for radio by Neville Teller* **based on the novel by Olga Hesky**

**Main Characters**

SHELLEY BERNSTEIN — Early 20s. New York American. Alert, bright but not superficial or shallow. Will probably turn into a very good business executive one day. Has heart. A warm tone to her voice. Probably falls in love with Tami on sight, but does not acknowledge it to herself until the hotel bedroom scene.

TAMI SHIMONI — 28. Israeli. Genuine, if light, Israeli accent essential. A cop with a poetic turn of mind – a man of action with a romantic centre. The softer element is always close to the surface, but we must believe that when called on to be tough, tough he will be.

PAPPA BARZILAI — Late 50s. Grizzled, tough old Israeli – take Prime Minister Shamir as a model. Genuine Israeli accent preferred – or a middle–European Yiddish if the genuine article is not available. Wily old bird. Must give impression of tremendous brain and nearly unlimited power – both worn very lightly.

170

\* \* \* \* \* \*

*(FULL UP EUROVISION SONG "HALLELUJAH" SUNG IN HEBREW. DOWN FOR OPENING ANNOUNCEMENT. UP MUSIC. CROSSFADE TO STEWARDESS ON DISTORT OVER BACKGROUND HUM OF AIRPLANE ENGINE)*

STEWARDESS:   Ladies and gentlemen, we are beginning our descent to Tel Aviv airport. Would you please fasten your seat belts and extinguish all cigarettes. Thank you.

JOSH:   Do you mind if I sit here for the landing? I prefer being near the front.

SHELLEY:   Help yourself.

JOSH:   You're an American.

SHELLEY:   Unmasked!

JOSH:   I thought so anyway. You can tell that band-box freshness a mile off.

SHELLEY:   Wow – a compliment... I think. And they told me all Israelis were rude. You are an Israeli, I take it?

JOSH:   I travel a lot. That makes the rough ways smooth, as the Bible puts it. By the way, I'm Yehoshua Caleb – Josh to you.

SHELLEY:   I'm Shelley Bernstein.

JOSH:   Shelley. I like it.

SHELLEY: I prefer the Hebrew version.

JOSH: Which is?

SHELLEY: Tzivya – or so my old grandma in the Bronx always told me.

JOSH: Shelley's fine. Been to Israel before?

SHELLEY: No, it's my first time. I'm on a round trip – London, Paris, Rome, Istanbul and Tel Aviv.

## (PLANE DESCENDING AND LANDING UNDER FOLLOWING)

JOSH: Sounds great.

SHELLEY: Tiring, but great. I'm being "finished", – American style. Last leg coming up then it's back to the family business. Cosmetics. Where have you been?

JOSH: I've also been on a sort of mini–tour. Then I hopped over to Istanbul to catch this flight. How long will you be staying in Israel?

SHELLEY: Two weeks. Why?

JOSH: I'd like to show you some of the sights. You know the Dead Sea, Masada, Lake Kinneret...

SHELLEY: Oh, I'll be joining a tour. Most of that's arranged.

JOSH:   Look, we'll be landing in a minute. Where are you staying?

SHELLEY:  We're in Tel Aviv for a few days. The Ramada.

JOSH:   I'll come and take you out tomorrow night – Saturday. We'll celebrate.

SHELLEY:  Celebrate? What?

JOSH:   Safe arrival. I'd come tonight, but there's nothing doing in Israel on the eve of the Sabbath. Expect me tomorrow at eight.

SHELLEY:  Hey, I'm not...

JOSH:   If I don't turn up it'll be *force majeur*. It really would be a crime not to keep a date with you. If I don't show, you must report it to the police.

SHELLEY:  *(laughs)* That'd be pushing it a bit.

### *(AIRPLANE ENGINE STOPS)*

JOSH:   No, I'm serious. I really mean it.

SHELLEY:   I can't think they'd consider it a crime worth investigating.

### *(STEWARDESS ON DISTORT)*

STEWARDESS:   Ladies and gentlemen, we have landed at Tel Aviv airport. The temperature outside is 27 degrees centigrade. We hope you've had a pleasant flight. Thank you.

**(HUM OF CONVERSATION AS PASSENGERS GET READY TO DISEMBARK)**

JOSH:    Here, let me help you with your things. Is this your coat?

SHELLEY:   Yes, it is. No, no – I won't wear it. Not in this heat.

JOSH:   These all yours?

SHELLEY:   Thank you.

JOSH:   I've got to go back for my hand luggage. You go on. Don't forget – eight o'clock tomorrow. See you Shelley, or Tzivya, or Rachel, or whoever you are.

SHELLEY:   Goodbye.

**(FADE OUT. FULL UP)**

TAMI :    That's how it all started – al least as far as I was concerned. Me? The name is Tami Shimoni. Inspector Tami Shimoni, to be precise, of the Tel Aviv police department. Just a cop – at least that's what I was when this thing all began. How did I get involved? Well, for one thing Caleb did not show up at the Ramada Hotel that Saturday night. Saturday evening in Tel Aviv – how can I describe it? From dusk on the eve of the Sabbath until the first star puts in an appearance in the Saturday evening sky, the whole town is pretty much like a morgue. Then slowly, one by one, the shops down the main thoroughfare – Dizengoff – switch on their lights and open their doors; the scores of cafés set out their tables and chairs on the wide boulevards;

### *(BRING UP CROWDS, TRAFFIC, CARS HOOTING)*

the traffic starts to flow – slowly at first, then faster and more furiously as daylight fades completely into the balmy summer night. And then the people. Whether they've spent the Sabbath in the synagogue or on the beach, out they come in ones and twos, in scores, and then in droves to sample the cosmopolitan delights of one of the world's great thoroughfares. The *Champs Elysées* of Israel. Amid all that noise, all those crowds, all that confusion, who could be expected to notice how it was that one young man toppled slowly to the pavement, blood spreading over his shirt front ...

WOMAN:  *(sudden scream)*

MAN 1:  Look out! He's hurt. Hold him...

### *(CROWD)*

WOMAN:  He's bleeding...

MAN 2:  Gently, gently.

MAN 1:  Get him into the cafe. This man's been hurt. Help me with him.

DR LIVNI:  Let me through. I'm a doctor.

SCHWARTZ:  In here. In here.

MAN 2:  Clear the way. Give us some room.

MAN 1:  Call the police, someone. For heaven's sake.

SCHWARTZ:   I've told someone, I've told someone. They'll be here soon. The station's only up the road. Through here – there's a sofa...

**(FULL UP CUTTING OVER BACKGROUND, HIGH PITCHED POLICE SIREN ON CAR AT HIGH SPEED. HOLD A MOMENT. FADE OUT. FADE IN – ECHO)**

SURGEON:   Dead on arrival I'm afraid, Inspector. Expert job. Blade clean through the heart. Don't suppose he even felt it. Pity. Nice looking young fellow.

TAMI:   Any lead on who he is, sergeant?

LIEB:   Not that I know. The boys upstairs may have something by now. Incidentally, did you notice the marks on his arms?

TAMI:   What marks?

LIEB:   There. Just inside the elbows. Those red spots.

TAMI:   That's odd. What do you think, Doc?

SURGEON:   Hypodermic, possibly.

LIEB:   What's odd? Dope. Stands to reason. After all, who gets knifed? Crooks. You wait till they've checked his prints. You'll see. A crook. I haven't been sitting round here for 20 years without learning a thing or two.

TAMI: Maybe. But only one mark on each arm? No – that must mean something. What, I wonder? Come on, sergeant, we're doing no good here. Let's see if the lab have anything.

### *(FADE OUT. FADE IN)*

TAMI: What do you mean negative?

YITZHAK: What does negative mean? Nothing. No evidence. Nothing on him, Tami. Nothing in his pockets, no money, no papers, no watch – not even a handkerchief. Every garment mass produced, all brand new. It's as though...

TAMI : As though he hadn't wanted us to find out who he was. Very disobliging. The Case of the Reluctant Corpse...

YITZHAK: So disobliging that he hasn't even favoured us with a stab wound through his shirt.

TAMI: Oh, Yitzhak, Yitzhak, what are you saying now?

YITZHAK: It's true. Look. Plenty of blood. No hole.

TAMI: It's a hot evening, for heaven's sake. Perhaps he had his shirt undone.

YITZHAK: I took it off him, it was buttoned up the front. Only the neck was undone.

TAMI: What does it mean?

YITZHAK: You're the detective, Tami. You work it out.

### (FADE OUT. FULL UP)

TAMI:    I walked home late that Saturday in the dust and the heat–smelling night. Down Dizengoff I walked, from the police station at the top end, and the streets were still crowded, far more than in daytime. The café tables stretched across the pavements almost to the road edge, jam–packed with people. In front of them, behind them, other crowds drifted, some shopping, some window shopping. Though Sunday would be an ordinary working day, no one was in a hurry to return to stifling apartments where it would be hard to sleep – not even me, drained after sixteen solid hours on duty.

Beyond the great raised square – the kikar – the crowds thinned, and 1 turned into the quieter residential street where I lodged. On the far corner was the lighted first floor window. Pappa Barzilai would be playing Chicaneuse with Mr Reuben. Mamma Barzilai would be in bed. She usually was, waited on hand and foot by Pappa. Lemon tea, hankies soaked in eau–de–cologne, books. She suffered from some mysterious ailment that innumerable doctors had failed to diagnose. Poor Pappa Barzilai's pay as some sort of clerk at Tel Aviv port couldn't really cover the cost of the daily help they had to employ, so my rent came in handy. I was lucky really. They'd practically adopted me.

### (KEY IN DOOR. DOOR OPENS)

PAPPA:    You won't believe it, Tami, he's another half a million shekels down. That's 45 million he owes me. When will he learn he can't trick me?

MR REUBEN:    Trick you? Who tries to trick you?

PAPPA:    You think I don't notice. I notice. But I don't let on. I see right through you and your little games. And don't think 1 won't collect that 45 million one day. I'll send a lawyer's letter.

MR REUBEN:  Lawyers – there won't be any need for lawyers. There won't be any 45 million. A run of bad luck, that's all I've had. It can happen to anyone. Goodnight, Shmuel. My luck will turn. You wait till tomorrow.

PAPPA:  I can wait.

MR REUBEN:  Goodnight, Tami.

TAMI:  Goodnight, Mr Reuben. Why on earth do you two play for such high stakes?

MR REUBEN:  It makes the game more exciting. Goodnight.

### (DOOR CLOSES)

PAPPA:  If he didn't try tricking me he'd do much better.

TAMI:  You know you wouldn't enjoy it half as much.

PAPPA:  You'd play a fair hand, Tami, if you put: your mind to it.

TAMI:  I'd rather put my mind to unarmed combat. Take up Chicaneuse with you? You've got a photographic memory to start off with. By the second time round you always know what card's coming next.

PAPPA:  And if I have? After all, what else have I got to occupy my mind? Only cards, and hearing about your job. Anything interesting kept you out so late today?

TAMI:  Nothing much... A chap goc himself bumped off in the middle of Dizengoff Street with a couple of thousand people round him – and no one saw a damn thing.

PAPPA:  Know who he was?

TAMI:  No idea. That's the snag. There wasn't a thing on him apart from his clothes. No marks except the knife wound.

PAPPA:  Hmm... Interesting. Wonder where he was killed,

TAMI:  Where he was... ? Of course! I must have been half asleep. That would explain the shirt – there wasn't any hole to correspond with the knife wound. He was dead when he arrived at Dizengoff. Probably unloaded from a car at the kerb, and supported on each side for a few paces. Then simply left·to fall – while the two of them walked away. That makes some sense of it all. It doesn't explain anything, but it makes some sense...

### *(FADE OUT. FADE IN)*

COHEN:  You won't believe it, Tami, but they've taken our corpse.

TAMI:  What do you mean, Super? Who's taken it?

COHEN:  There's something up. It's no use asking me – I don't know.

TAMI:  But who took it?

COHEN: I told you – I don't know. I can guess, but I don't know. Anyway, there was an order from the Inspector General this morning. We're to carry on with routine enquiries.

TAMI: Without a corpse? Super! Are they going to tell us who it is? They obviously know.

COHEN: If I know the form, they'll tell us nothing. We carry on with routine enquiries, and in a day or two we'll be told to forget it, the case is closed.

TAMI: For heaven's sake…

COHEN: I know. But for the moment we carry on. You'd better see the two witnesses the squad boys reported in. An old doctor sitting outside the cafe, and the cafe owner. The rest of them ran like hell when they were asked to give information.

TAMI: OK, we've got witnesses of a sort. But what about the body?

COHEN: There's been a post mortem – that 1 know by the grace of Sergeant Lieb. Done in the middle of the night and all very hush–hush. No word of what was or wasn't found.

TAMI: Who were the hush–hush boys? Sergeant Lieb recognise them?

COHEN: If he did he's not saying.

TAMI: Shin Bet, perhaps? It could be a Counter-Intelligence job. Or Military Security?

COHEN: May be. Or...

TAMI: Or?

COHEN: Nothing, Tami – forget it. Anyway your name's on the docket, so you go through the motions. The media may be after you, but you know nothing, see?

TAMI: I do know nothing.

COHEN: Less than nothing, then. Go on, you see those witnesses. There's only one other call, and you can have your half day.

TAMI: What's this, then? Just a simple bank robbery?

COHEN: No, no, nothing like that. A tourist at the Ramada Hotel says she's been robbed.

TAMI: What about somebody else for a change?

COHEN: Everybody else is as busy as a left–handed beigel – maker.

TAMI: *(hollow laugh)* Can't the tourist wait?

COHEN: No. she has to leave Tel Aviv – she's with a party. It's your pigeon because you're the best English speaker round here. No, you make those calls. write your reports, and off you go – free till tomorrow.

TAMI: Thank you for nothing.

**(FADE OUT. FADE IN)**

DR LIVNI:   Fifty years ago we came to this country. I'd only just qualified as a doctor back in "der haim" – what is now Rumania. I've lived through everything – '48, '67, '72. Now I've retired. Almost retired – I still see a private patient or two, you know. But I live very quietly now my dear wife has passed on. A few friends, a swim every morning, winter and summer – and on Saturday nights I go and sit at a cafe table – always the same one – and watch the crowds go by.

TAMI:   And last Saturday night, Dr Livni?

DR LIVNI:   As usual. I was sitting at my table, and the waiters were putting more and more tables in front, when I noticed three men...

TAMI:   What made you notice specially?

DR LIVNI:   It somehow looked strange –three heads, quite close together, moving through the crowds.

TAMI:   What happened next?

DR LIVNI:   Well, suddenly all the people walking in front of us seemed to bunch together. I stood up to see what was going on, but I couldn't see anything except that there was someone on the ground. Then there was a scream, more pushing backwards and forwards, and then they were carrying someone into the café past me. I called out I was a doctor, and they let me through. The young man was dead when I got to him.

TAMI:   Was he warm?

DR LIVNI:   Warm? Of course, he must have been. He was just dead, wasn't he?

TAMI:   Yes. Yes, of course. And the other two? Would you recognise them again? Could you identify them?

DR LIVNI:   No, I don't think so… It was only the heads I saw. Dark heads.

TAMI:   Did you see where they came from? Did you see a car pull up to the kerb just before?

DR LIVNI:   There might have been. But 1 wouldn't have noticed, unless there was some special reason.

TAMI:   Well, thank you very much. You've been very helpful. Goodbye, Dr Livni.

DR LIVNI:   Goodbye. Let me show you out. Will you be needing me again. Inspector?

TAMI:   I doubt it, doctor. That's a striking photograph.

DR LIVNI:   My son. He died. The Six Day War. On the last day.

TAMI:   Oh…. I'm sorry.

DR LIVNI:   You're like him. Very much like. I noticed it at once.

**(FADE OUT. FULL UP)**

TAMI: I wasn't though. Like his son, I mean. I reckon he saw his son in every young man he met. He waved at me as I walked down the garden. His son should have been there – to pull up the cactuses and plant some flowers. It was 10.30. My next call was the café owner.

.The Cafe Schwartz in Dizengoff was empty. Outside there were a few breakfasters or early–morning coffee drinkers, but inside in the light of day the chrome plastic-topped tables and imitation marble walls were depressingly aseptic. The espresso machine bubbled and winked malignant red and green signals. Behind it loomed its master, Nahum Schwartz, his face carved from stone.

### (FADE UP BUBBLINC ESPRESSO MACHINE. OCCASIONAL DISTANT TRAFFIC)

SCHWARTZ: Another of you. Nothing better to do? I told your people everything I know last night. And that's nothing. It's still the same.

TAMI: Someone is murdered in the busiest part of town and you want us to do nothing? Especially when there's a trained observer on the spot?

SCHWARTZ: Where do you get that 'trained observer'? I don't poke my nose into other people's affairs.

TAMI: You've been in this business too long not to know a thing or two. I bet you could pick up the villains quicker than most police-men on the force.

SCHWARTZ: Wouldn't say that. I don't entertain crooks – never did, not even when I had that caff down in the Jaffa port area.

TAMI: I didn't mean that. But all kinds come here. Wasn't there maybe someone you recognised? That you remember, perhaps, from years back? At any time in the evening? It might have nothing to do with this affair, but it could give us a lead.

SCHWARTZ: You ever been here on a Saturday night? Know what it's like?

WAITER: *(approaching)* Two espressos.

**(CUPS, MACHINE)**

SCHWARTZ: Is that all?

WAITER: It's all they ordered.

SCHWARTZ: Offer them the cake. Twenty people could get themselves killed under your nose, and you wouldn't be any wiser.

TAMI: Twenty corpses.

SCHWARTZ: Yes, well. I didn't see the dead man till they'd brought him in, and I'd never seen him before, that I can tell you. A nice panic it made in here, turning my cafe into a morgue. Ruined my night's business.

TAMI: I'm sure he'd have been very upset about that. Most inconsiderate.

SCHWARTZ: It's all right for you. You get your wages, come what. In fact, the more corpses the better, eh?

TAMI: Not exactly. So you saw nothing. Couldn't have, I suppose, since you were inside here when it all happened.

SCHWARTZ: Well...

TAMI: You weren't?

SCHWARTZ: I wasn't inside and I wasn't outside. I was standing in the door and looking to see if I could squeeze in an extra table.

TAMI: You saw the man fall, then?

SCHWARTZ: No, I didn't. I saw heads bobbing about. Thought someone had fainted – that sort of thing.

TAMI: And before that? Maybe you recognised someone? Some passer–by?

SCHWARTZ: Well.... Well, it won't help you. He'd gone on before it all happened. He was well in front of the dead man. But there was this character. Haven't seen him around for years. Remember thinking to myself: "Thought you were dead and gone." I don't even know his real name. Hashi, they used to call him – expect he had something to do with hashish. Small–time, I'd reckon. Anyway, I do know the law caught up with him years ago in Jaffa.

TAMI: And you saw this... character ... just where in relation to the dead man?

SCHWARTZ: Nowhere in relation. That's you all over, all of you!
Putting words into people's mouths. I said it was before all that. I just caught sight of him. He was looking round. Maybe he'd seen or

heard something. Then he was gone. I never gave it another thought till you asked me just now.

**_(FADE OUT. FULL UP)_**

TAMI : 11.15. Only the American tourist to see now, and a couple of reports. Prospects for my half day were definitely bright. The Ramada Hotel is one of a half dozen that rise, monolithic, on the seaward side of Tel Aviv's promenade. If it has any distinguishing feature, it is that it projects a shade more defiantly than most towards the sea, while from its townward face, honeycombed with balconies like a hive for giant bees, a glass doored portico leads into a lobby chilled to freezing.

**_(FADE UP HOTEL LOBBY)_**

Police. You have a guest by name Bernstein? Miss Bernstein?

CLERK: Just a minute. Yes. Room 210. You can phone from here.

TAMI: Thanks.

**_(DIALLING. SHELLEY ON DISTORT)_**

SHELLEY: Hello.

TAMI: Miss Bernstein? Miss Shelley Bernstein?

SHELLEY: Yes. Who is this?

TAMI: Tel Aviv police. You reported a theft.

SHELLEY:   Oh yes. At last. I'd given you up.

TAMI:   Sorry. I didn't want to call too early. I'm down in the hotel lobby.

SHELLEY:   Shall I come down?

TAMI:   If you don't mind.

### (OFF HOTEL BACKGROUND)

As I put the phone down I seemed, out of the corner of my eye, to catch a movement, too vague to be sure about. 1 glanced up. A couple of women strolling towards the doors, a man standing by the elevators. Waiting for someone to come down, of course. He was turned away so I couldn't see his face, but that was the way he would be. Anyway, who could possibly be interested in my call on an insignificant tourist? And then one of the elevators disgorged a small huddle of people. A nondescript man; a middle–aged couple – the woman in a white straw hat that was standard for British tourists, the man wearing a heavy jacket; a grey–haired woman who could be nothing but a schoolmistress – and a remarkably pretty girl exuding a sort of vitamin-fed sparkle that could only be American. I kept my eyes on the schoolmistress. She must be Miss Bernstein. With my luck she had to be. But no...

### (UP HOTEL BACKGROUND)

CLERK:   Miss Bernstein.

SHELLEY:   Are you from the police? You don't look like my idea of a policeman.

TAMI: Would you like my identification?

SHELLEY: Not necessary. Shall we sit down? You must be from the police or you wouldn't know about my complaint, would you?

TAMI: Quite.

SHELLEY: *(exasperated)* Oh, how British that sounds!

TAMI: You expected to come here and find a collection of caricatures, waving their hands about? How very disappointing for you.

SHELLEY: My, my! We do have a chip on our shoulder, don't we?
What's your name?

TAMI: There you go again. That's what I ought to be asking you.

SHELLEY: But you know it. And 1 can't go on calling you "you".

TAMI: I'm Inspector Tami Shimoni.

SHELLEY: Inspector! Aren't you rather young for that?

TAMI: Sorry to disappoint you again, but Inspector's the lowest form of life for a plain clothes man. Our ranks don't go the same as yours. And I'm not as young as I look. Now, let's get down to it, shall we?

SHELLEY: All right. Would you like some coffee?

TAMI:    No thank you. Now, something was stolen from you, Miss Bernstein. What was it, and where did it happen?

SHELLEY:   It was a camera. As for where – I don't know.

TAMI:   An expensive camera? What make?

SHELLEY:   Not expensive. As a matter of fact it was very cheap. That's what makes it so odd. Anyone could have seen it wasn't worth stealing. But that wasn't why... at least, not altogether why... I called the police. *(pause)* Look, I'm not making much sense, am I? Let me tell it all from the beginning. I arrived here on Friday. I'm on a round trip here for two weeks. I got on at Istanbul. It was one of those big jets – you know, three seats one side, two the other. 1 took a window seat and the one next to me was empty. As we were starting the descent a young man came and sat next to me. Said he wanted to be near the front for the landing...

TAMI:   Not surprising, whatever he said.

SHELLEY:   I don't think it was just interest. Oh, he was interested – but there seemed more to it. He seemed kind of... pressed, anxious. He was talking to me, but half his mind was on something else.

TAMI:   What did you talk about?

SHELLEY:   He asked if this was my first trip to Israel. Then he said he'd like to show me around some...

TAMI:   He was an Israeli, then?

SHELLEY:   I guess so. He didn't exactly say. Then the plane began to dip, and he asked where I was staying. I saw no reason not to tell him, and he said he'd call on Saturday night and take me out. Something about celebrating. Then he said something odd. He said that if he didn't show, I was to tell the police because it would be a crime to stand me up. Well, I laughed that off, and then when we'd landed he helped me with my things, and even tried to help me on with my coat, though it was terrifically hot so I didn't let him. And that was that.

TAMI:   Was that the last you saw of him?

SHELLEY:   Yes. Well, except that I did see him crossing to the airport building, but by then there were a couple of people walking back with him, so he must have had some friends on the plane.

TAMI:   And the camera?

SHELLEY:   The camera – it had been in my coat pocket, you see. I only noticed it was gone this morning when I was getting my things ready to go to Jerusalem. I didn't know quite what to do, really... And then I phoned the police.

TAMI:   I see. And it was this young man who took the camera?

SHELLEY:   I suppose it must have been.

TAMI:   And his name7 Did he tell you?

SHELLEY:   Yes he did. Yehoshua Caleb. He said to call him Josh.

TAMI:   So what did you really call us about then? To tell us about the camera – or the non–appearance of your boy friend?

SHELLEY: *(furious)* He was not my boy friend. And I don't need the police to look for dates that stand me up.

TAMI: I didn't mean...

SHELLEY: I don't give a good red hoot what you mean. And if that's your idea of a joke here in Israel – what he did – then I don't care for your sense of humour any more than for your policemen. And as for the camera, you can forget it.

### *(FADE OUT. FULL UP)*

TAMI: End of a beautiful friendship – before it had even begun.

When you step outside the ferocious air conditioning and the shaded lobbies of these modern Tel Aviv hotels, the heat and the sunlight hit you like a blow. I'd just turned to where I'd left the car, when I felt a real hand on my shoulder, firmly steering me to where a large black car was double parked.

### *(FADE UP TRAFFIC)*

Hey, what's this?

UZI: You Tami Shimoni?

TAMI: Yes. Who the hell are you? What do you want?

UZI: You, old man. You come with me.

TAMI: I'll do no such thing. Be careful, I'm a police officer.

UZI: I know you're a police officer. I'm a colleague – in a way. Look.

TAMI: That's a forgery. I know every detective inspector on this force – and you're not one of them.

UZI: No, but it saves a lot of explaining. I'm from GUG. You know about GUG, 1 take it?

TAMI: GUG – Roof. The umbrella organisation for state intelligence operations.

UZI: That's right. We tackle all the things the other security services won't dirty their–hands with. You do know.

TAMI: But...

UZI: What do you expect? A silver badge? Are you getting into that car, or am I going to have to make you?

TAMI: I'll come, I'll come.

### (CAR DOOR OPENS)

UZI: In there.

### (CAR INTERIOR. CAR DOOR CLOSES)

Step on it, Yossi.

### (LIMOUSINE ENGINE FROM WITHIN CAR
### MOVES UP TO SPEED)

What are you looking at your watch for? You got something planned for this afternoon?

TAMI:  My half day. I'd fixed something up.

UZI:  Too bad.

**(UP ENGINE. HOLD A BIT. CAR COMES TO A HALT)**

Out!

**(CAR DOORS OPEN AND CLOSE. OPEN AIR, FOOTSTEPS)**

TAMI:  What's this, then? Customs sheds? We're at the port, aren't we?

UZI:  Don't ask..

**(KNOCK AT DOOR. DOOR OPENS)**

In you go. Inspector Shimoni.

PAPPA:  Ah, Tami . Come in, come in!

TAMI:  *(incredulous)* Pappa? Pappa Barzilai? What on earth...?

PAPPA:  Close the door, Tami And close your mouth. You look like a stranded fish.

TAMI:  Sorry, sorry.

**(DOOR CLOSES)**

But what are you doing here?

PAPPA:   What do you think I'm doing? Working!

TAMI:   But you're...

PAPPA:   But I'm the last person you'd expect to find in this chair.
Is that it? Even though you know I come to the port every day. Exactly. It's really very good cover. Sit down, Tami, sit down. You're making the place look untidy. Now, first of all, don't be angry.

TAMI:   Angry? Yes, well. No—one likes being fooled, I suppose. Why did you suddenly decide to let me in on it now?

PAPPA:   I always meant to have you in with us sooner or later, you know. But there's always the right moment. Now is the time for you to come in. We need you.

TAMI:   Why me?

PAPPA:   I'll come to that. First, do you know what GUG is?

TAMI:   Only that it's a roof organisation for the security services.

PAPPA:   That's good enough. We coordinate the work of the other three agencies when necessary – that is, the police, Shin Bet and Military Intelligence. And we function in ways the others can't. The real power of this organisation that I... control... comes from the fact that I am nobody. Hardly anyone knows about me, and my authority comes from a source that wouldn't acknowledge me even if challenged. The other agencies are run by people in the public eye.

Either they, or the Minister responsible for them, have to answer for what they do, even when the truth may destroy our security, for thank heavens we live in a Parliamentary democracy. But since they have to take the rap when something goes very wrong. they're sometimes – being only human – reluctant to take risks which have to be taken. I, though... I don't need to answer any questions, because nobody would think of asking me. And as for taking the blame – well, that's my job. Someone has to be the garbage remover.

TAMI:   Don't you have a boss, then?

PAPPA:   Oh yes... in a way. But I have to make up my own mind how the garbage is removed. I've one advantage. I get the cooperation of the other three services. That's my price for doing the dirty work that they can then be quite innocent about. Now, why do I want you? The reason, Tami, is that you're already in to something we're busy with.

TAMI:   The dead man in Dizengoff Street?

PAPPA:   Yes – and no.

TAMI:   I'm not really into it, you know. Not since they – it must have been you – had him taken away from us. Was he one of yours?

PAPPA:   He was, yes. We hadn't known he was back in Israel.
But the fact that he was killed, and left for us to find, told us a great deal.

TAMI:   But where do I come into all this?

PAPPA:   You'll understand in a minute. But first I'll have to tell you about some things. There aren't very many who know them. And frankly, even now I'm going to say as little as I can. You've heard perhaps about the German scientists working in Libya.

TAMI: Only what's in the papers. They're making rockets, aren't they?

PAPPA: Rockets, schmockets!

TAMI: But aren't they? Everyone knows...

PAPPA: They were – but that lot's gone home now. The job's finished. No, there's something else being made there now – more horrible and more deadly than any weapon that's ever been used.

TAMI: What is it?

PAPPA: That, unfortunately, is what we don't know. Probably some kind of micro–virus, something they dreamed up, invented all by themselves. One of their geniuses was a little indiscreet – wrote a letter home, couldn't help boasting. He said there was no antidote, except one made from the same formula. I don't understand these things, but that seemed to make sense to the backroom boys. The man you saw yesterday – in the morgue – had been there to find out what it was. And he did.

TAMI: Then you know!

PAPPA: No. We got a signal from his partner, but it wasn't clear. Apparently he had a sample with him. That sample was his death warrant.

TAMI: They got it back from him?

PAPPA:   I'm almost certain they didn't. If they had, we'd never have found the body.

TAMI:   But Pappa, I don't see...

PAPPA:   You will. This is what must have happened. Once he'd got hold of that sample, his first problem was to get himself out of Libya as fast as he could. He caught a plane –the first available. It happened to be going to Istanbul.

TAMI:   Istanbul! Then he was the man...

PAPPA:   Exactly. He was the mysterious Joshua Caleb who sat next to your American tourist. By the way, Tami, doesn't the name tell you something?

TAMI:   That's funny... there *was* something about 1 couldn't quite...

PAPPA:   Try this. I don't exactly remember the words, but "... from the tribe of Judah, Caleb the son of ..." somebody or other. Then "...from the tribe of Ephraim, Yehoshua the son of Nun."

TAMI:   The spies sent out by Moses to reconnoitre the Promised Land!

PAPPA:   Yes. It's a bit of romantic tomfoolery, but since the boys have to have cover names, we choose them from that bunch. We've got a female list, too.

TAMI:   But he gave Miss Bernstein both names – Joshua and Caleb.

PAPPA: I'm afraid that's a bad sign. It means Caleb is dead, too. Joshua must have known that his chances of getting to us were pretty slim, that they'd be waiting for him.

TAMI: No Pappa, they were on the plane with him.

PAPPA: Ah?

TAMI: Miss Bernstein noticed that he seemed nervous. Then later she saw him going across the tarmac with two other people. She assumed they were friends. They must have been on the plane with him. Why on earth didn't he ask someone – anyone – for help?

PAPPA: It wasn't one of our planes, Tami. How could he know who to trust?

TAMI: He trusted her.

PAPPA: No, he didn't. He didn't trust anybody. This is too big, too important. Everything, all our lives, the lives of everyone in Israel, depends on it. Some risk he had to take. He must have been pretty sure that he'd never to us alive, so he did the get best he could. He chose an American girl, travelling alone, and tried to make sure that she'd get some word to us. Stealing that camera was the best he could improvise. Joshua wanted us to find Miss Shelley Bernstein. He did very well. I hope Miss Bernstein takes your fancy or rather, that you take hers. You're going to be pretty close for the next few days.

TAMI: But she's already told me everything.

PAPPA: She hasn't, Tami. Maybe she told you everything she thinks she knows. But there must be more. There has to be more. If not, the alternative is... unthinkable.

TAMI:   You're quite sure they ... the other side didn't get that sample back from Joshua?

PAPPA:  Pretty positive. They dumped that body so that we could get after the stuff before the trail got too cold. They'll be watching – and we'll be doing their work for them.

TAMI:   Those marks on Joshua's arms. Truth serum?

PAPPA:  They tried, but there wouldn't have been time. He was a trained agent. No, they got nothing out of him, so they killed him and dumped the body in the most public place they could think of.

TAMI:   But Pappa, as soon as we concentrate on the girl Shelley Bernstein – that'll be just what they're waiting for. They'll move in. She'll be in real danger.

PAPPA:  She'd be their first choice anyway. They know Joshua was sitting next to her on the plane. You'd better get moving. And don't go home, go straight after her. By the way, contact nobody – nobody at all – except me.

TAMI:   How shall I do that?

PAPPA:  By phone, of course. What do you think? Phone old Pappa Barzilai, at home or at his office at the port. Now, there's a car ready for you near the gate. It looks like one of the police regulars, but if you need a turn of speed you'll notice the difference. There's a bag in it, packed. Your super's been told you're getting a short leave – private reasons. He'll probably guess the truth, but guesses hatch no eggs. Hand over your wallet.

TAMI: My wallet? What for?

PAPPA: Here's another – not so very different. But look, if you hold it against the light... see that embossed design?

TAMI: The letter 'Gimmel'?

PAPPA: Gimmel for GUG. Identification if you need it.
Oh – 20,000 shekels. Government money. To be accounted for, but used without qualms when necessary. Now, you're Inspector Tami Shimoni of the Israeli Police, Tel Aviv Branch, and you're taking a bit of leave to make time with an attractive tourist you happened to meet while on duty...
Right ?

TAMI: Right.

PAPPA: If it's any comfort, there'll be someone or other of mine fairly near you all the time – though you'd better play this as though you didn't know it. Well, get going.

TAMI: Yes... yes, I'd better.

PAPPA: *(calls)* Oh, and don't bother going back to the Ramada Hotel. I got a message while you were on your way. She's left for Jerusalem to catch up with the rest of her tour – they'll be sight–seeing in Mea Shearim at four.

TAMI: Jerusalem. it is, then. I'm on my way.

### *(FADE OUT. FULL UP; CAR ENGINE BENEATH, OCCASIONALLY REVVING INTO LOWER GEAR AND BACK AGAIN)*

TAMI:   For the first half of the hour–long drive from Tel Aviv to Jerusalem I was in a kind of mental maze.

I kept starting down little avenues of thought, only to come hard up against a blank wall of wonder at what I'd learned. It was only when the wide motorway narrowed down to begin the long, winding ascent to Jerusalem that the full import of what had happened hit me. The road runs between the rearing golden heads of mountains which face each other across wide–valleys; they stand aloof and invincible, just as they have stood guarding the stronghold for thousands of years. It was that long, long story of conquest and revolt that suddenly brought home to me what the country, close–ringed with enemies, now faced. Extinction – for everyone. It could happen – but it mustn't. For the thing that Joshua had brought back with him was the key – and it was still here, in Israel.. Those who had killed him had not succeeded in getting it back. They mustn't.

I rounded the last upward curve of the long climb, and the city of Jerusalem gleaned and shimmered in the heat, the sun transmuting to gold the yellow stones of its buildings. I glanced at my watch. A minute after four. I beat the first traffic lights and drove straight down towards Mea Shearim.

Mea Shearim, the ultra–orthodox district of the city, is not very large, and 1 saw the Oceanic Tours coach at once, waiting empty in a sort of courtyard. Beyond lay the warren of alleys and passages where, in a self–imposed ghetto, the highly religious recreate the conditions their forefathers fled from in Europe. The touring party was obviously being shown over the religious school – the "yeshiva." – that ran along one side of the courtyard.

### (CAR STOPS. DOOR OPENS AND CLOSES)

As I parked the car the group began emerging. I reached the entrance at the moment Shelley Bernstein came out, blinking, in to the sunlight.

## (FADE UP GROUP)

SHELLEY:  You!

TAMI:  Me. I hope you don't mind?

SHELLEY:  I mind. What are you doing here? Following me? Haven't you anything better to do?

TAMIi:  Not at the moment.

MAX:  Gather round, ladies and gentlemen. We shall be moving off in a minute to the University campus.

SHELLEY: *(whisper)* 1 think it's a disgrace.

MAX:  … the Hebrew University, that is.

TAMI:  *(whisper)* What is?

MAX:  You may not know that the University is on two sites – one on Mount Scopus to the east of the city…

SI1ELLEY:  *(whisper)* A public servant with nothing better to do.

MAX: … and the new campus to the west, facing Israel's Parliament – the Knesset – on the opposite hill.

TAMI: *(whisper)* Sh–sh! Listen!

MAX: That's where we'll be going. We'll drive along the Jaffa road, past the central bus station., and round to the university. Afterwards we'll complete the circle back to the King David Hotel in good time for you to change for dinner.

FREDA: *(calls)* Is there much walking? I don't think 1 can take much more.

MAX: There is some, Mrs Harrison, but you can stay in the coach if you prefer.

FREDA: Would you mind, Joe? My feet are killing me.

JOE: Wait till we get there. You might feel better.

MAISIE: I'll stay with you, if you like, Mrs Harrison.

FREDA: Would you?

JOE: All right, you two can have a natter. Mr Rice will come with me – eh, Mr Rice? You don't mind leaving your wife with mine, do you?

HYMIE: – Hymie. And it'll be a pleasure.

MAISIE: I heard that, Hymie.

MAX: Right. Back in the coach everyone, please. Time is moving on.

SHELLEY: You're not proposing to tag along, surely?

TAMI: Well, now I'm here. I've never seen the new university, I'll juse follow the coach.

SHELLEY: Well – really!

***(FADE OUT. FADE IN TELEPHONE RINING ON DISTORT – ISRAELI TONE. RECEIVER LIFTED PAPPA ON DISTORT)***

TAMI: It's me. Tami.

PAPPA: Ah, Tami. How are you? We got your message that you'd be away for a couple of days. Where are you? Jerusalem?

TAMI: Yes.

PAPPA: Which hotel?

TAMI: The King David.

PAPPA: Very nice, too. Hope you manage to enjoy yourself a bit. Or is it all work?

TAMI: That's what I wanted…

PAPPA: Hot, is it? So it is here. Just a minute – Mamma says you want to be careful – it gets cold there in the evenings. Put something on, she says. *(calls)* You go back, Mamma. I'll bring your lemon tea when the kettle boils. *(pause – then low)* Now quickly, Tami, what's the trouble?

TAM I The trouble is, I'm getting nowhere. And I don't see how I can unless I can tell the girl at least something. She either feels persecuted, or thinks I'm some sort of Lothario. She resents it.

PAPPA:  *(chuckles)* You're slipping, Tami. Look, remember that place we had an ice–cream last time we went on a trip to Jerusalem – about half–way?

TAMI:  I remember.

PAPPA:  See you there, then. About forty minutes.

### *(FADE OUT. FADE IN)*

ARTZI:  Wasn't too difficult, super. Got on to him through his wife – or that's what she used to call herself, before they split up. He's still working the Jaffa market.

COHEN:  The elusive Hashi, eh? Well sergeant, *did* Nahum Schwartz see him last Saturday night?

ARTZI:  Didn't ask him, super. Thought I d best leave it to you.

COHEN:  You'd better wheel him in, then.

ARTZI:  Sir.

### *(DOOR OPENS)*

*(calls)* Bring him in. You – stand there.

COHEN:  You normally known as Hashi?

207

HASHI:   That's what they call me. Doesn't mean anything.

COHEN:   Not now, maybe. Go back a few years, though...

HASHI:   A few? Ten! Ten years, and straight as a die.

COHEN:   Oh yes? *(pause)* You were in Dizengoff Street on Saturday night.

HASHI:   And if I was. That's no crime.

COHEN:   But there was a crime. Murder is a crime. Or didn't you know?

HASHI:   I ask you, isn't that just like the cops? Here's a man – a reformed character, a straight citizen –and all they can do is pull him in every time he's in the neighbourhood of something crooked. Easier than looking for who done it...

COHEN:   All right, all right. No–one's accusing you of anything – yet. But we do know you saw something, and we want to know what.

HASHI:   I should say no–one's accusing me. Nothing to accuse me of. I'm an honest citizen.

COHEN:   Well, honest citizen, you can prove it by cooperating with the police. Now, you were walking along, just going past the Cafe Schwartz, when you looked back, over your shoulder, and you saw – what?

HAStil:   Since you know it all ... all right, all right.

That's all there was to it. Walking along, doing no one any harm, when I looked round – don't even know why. And there behind me I saw this face – could have sworn the chap was dead already. That's what it looked like. And then I saw he must have been, because this couple let go of him. Naturally, not wanting to get mixed up in anything not my business, off I went a bit sharpish.

COHEN:   These two you saw letting the man go – I'm interested in them.

HASHI:   Them? They were just an ordinary looking couple, quite ordinary…

### *(FADE OUT. FULL UP)*

TAMI:    The place that Pappa Barzilai fixed for a rendezvous was a café in a service station, about half–way between Tel Aviv and Jerusalem. When I got down, I found the place dimly lit and deserted in the slack evening hour. But the old man was already there, calm and unhurried, as if he'd been sitting at the table for hours.

### *(FADE IN)*

PAPPA:   I've ordered a lemon tea. What'll you have, Tami?

TAMI:   I'll have a lemon squash.

PAPPA:   *(calls)* And one lemon squash.

WAITRESS:   *(calls)* on the way.

PAPPA:   I've been thinking over what you said. I can see it might help to tell the girl something of the story. But is she to be trusted?

TAM1: Trusted? What do you mean?

PAPPA: Tami, you haven't thought this through. As far as your end of the affair is concerned, we've been acting on her story of what happened in the plane.
Right?

TAMI: Ye–es...

PAPPA: Well, that's her story. Hasn't it occurred to you that it may never have happened? Or not that way at all?

TAMI: But then why...?

PAPPA: Yes, that's the question. Except for what she told us, we don't even know that Joshua did return on that particular plane. Oh, he came into the country that Friday on one of his passports – we have that from immigration – but not necessarily with Miss Bernstein. But even if he were on the same plane. suppose he hadn't managed to dispose of what he was carrying? Couldn't she be providing us with a nice diversion and putting us on the wrong track altogether?

TAMI: I don't believe it.

PAPPA: I don't believe it. Ah!

### (CUPS. GLASSES)

WAITRESS: One lemon tea. One lemon squash.

PAPPA: Thank you. But you do see that it's a possibility, don't you? Still, since we both consider it unlikely we can come to a compromise. You can tell her about Joshua – that he was one of our boys. No need to mentlon GUG, of course. That he'd tried to give her something – we don't know what – or a message, to hand on to us. And that it's vitally important we find it before some... some others.

TAMI:  Yes, that'll help. I'm sure it will. By the way, do you know anything about some of these other people in the group? There could easily be a couple of them among the rest – perhaps the ones that were on the plane with Joshua.

PAPPA:  We're working on it, Tami. Have you noticed anyone acting... out of character?

TAl,'iI:  There's one couple:  a wiry–looking woman with a doggy face; husband bald and tanned. Healthy type.

PAPPA:  He's a golfer – hobby, not profession. They're named Harrison. He's Joe, she's Freda. They're from California – at least that's what their passports say.
He's the manager of some trust company.

TAMI:  How did you get all that so soon?

PAPPA:  Mainly the guide. He's a friend of ours – believes we're Shin Bet, I think. In case you need him, tell him Hirschfeld sent you.

TAMI:  Who's Hirschfeld?

PAPPA:  No idea. But the chap who recruited him thought he'd appreciate a little cloak and dagger.

### (FADE OUT. FULL UP)

TAMI:  I drove back to Jerusalem, the night rushing past, punctuated with the bright sparks of insects' wings caught briefly in the car headlights. They whirled past or smashed against the windscreen. Soon the mountain ahead was outlined against the city's glow, and then I was looking across the valley into the thousand pin–points of light – a sparkle of jewels on the Jerusalem hills, strung about with necklaces of yellow street lamps. Into the town I drove, skirting the Jaffa gate that led into the old walled city, and so back to the King David Hotel on the opposite hillside. I looked at my watch, thinking it must be about midnight. I could scarcely believe it when I saw the hands standing at 8.30. On the terrace the white–clothed tables each had a festive red candle burning in a glass chimney. I looked round. She was sitting at the far side, her back to me – but there was no mistaking that smooth curtain of hair. She wasn't alone. The Harrisons were with her.

**(FADE UP CONVERSATION, CROCKERY, BACKGROUND MUSIC)**

SHELLEY:  You!

TAMI:  You say that whenever you see me. My name is Tami – try that next time. Sounds more friendly.

SHELLEY:  What are you doing here?

TAMI:  Staying here, at the hotel. Hoping to have dinner now. May I sit with you?

SHELLEY:  If you must. Joe and Freda Harrison, this is Inspector Tami Shimoni. He's a policeman.

FREDA:   A policeman!

JOE:   Nice to meet you, Inspector.

TAMI:   Mr. Harrison. Mrs Harrison.

SHELLEY:   Are you following me?

TAMI:   I'm having a bit of a vacation. Even policemen are human – they need time off, too. Is there a better way to spend it, than following a pretty girl?

FREDA:   A Jewish policeman! Just fancy! Oh, Mr Shimoni, I know it sounds silly to you but it's wonderful to us. Gives us such a thrill.

JOE:   Are you a sabra, Mr Shimoni?

TAMI:   No, I wasn't born here.

JOE:   Where do you come from, then? Which country?

TAMI:   Russia. My father was a refusenik in the 1960s.
He applied to emigrate to Israel, so he was thrown out of his job in the university. He went on applying for 5 years, but he became very ill. In the end they gave us permission, but before we could leave he died. So I came here with my mother. But it was all too much for her – the shock of his death, coming to a new country. She couldn't cope. She developed some sort of depression and had to go into hospital. So I was sent to a children's village. That's where I was brought up.

FREDA:   An orphanage? You poor thing!

TAMI:   Oh no, not really. It was nothing like that. It was a good place. We looked on the teachers as parents – sort of communal mothers and fathers.

FREDA:   And your own mother?

TAMI:   She died – about eight years ago. But I never felt deprived. 1 was the youngest in the village for quite a few years, so 1 reckon I was spoilt more than a little.

SHELLEY:   That accounts for it.

JOE:   Your English is very good. Where did you learn it?

TAMI:   At the village at first. The school was excellent.
Then a couple of years ago 1 was sent to England for some special training. I was there more than a year.

FREDA:   It must be an exciting life.

TAMI:   Oh it is, Mrs Harrison. One gets involved in all sorts of exotic crimes. Like camera stealing from tourists.

SHELLEY:   Sarcasm.

MAISIE:   *(approaching)* Freda, my dear! How are the feet?

FREDA:   Hello Maisie. Ghastly – like they've been cut off at the ankle. I can't feel them. It's those foot salts the hotel druggist recommended – it's made them go all numb. I'm not sure if I prefer them this way, or throbbing like they were before.

MAISIE:   I must get some. My feet are all swollen.

JOE:   I told you not to be so lavish with them, Freda. Now see what you've done. Don't let her go wild with them, Hymie.

HYMIE:   Do I care if she can feel her feet or not?

SHELLEY:   Let me introduce you.
Inspector Shimoni – Mr and Mrs Rice.

HYMIE:   } Nice to know you.

MAISIE:   } Pleased to meet you

TAMI:   How do you do?

MAISIE:   Well, we've got a table booked over there. We're having dinner with that nice Miss Stoddart. She's a headmistress you know. Retired this year and taking the holiday she's always dreamed of. She's a really interesting person.

SHELLEY:   Yes, I like her.

MAISIE:   Be seeing you then. Bye!

FREDA:   Goodbye.

SHELLEY:   You know, 1 really think 1 ought to be going up to bed. I promised myself an early night. We're off very early in the morning.

TAMI:   So you are. For Beer–Sheva and the Negev.

SHELLEY:   That's right.

TAMI: Funnily enough I'm off there, too.

SHELLEY: Whatever for.

TAMI: To see a man about a camel.

SHELLEY: Oh well, 1 can't stop you. Excuse me, I'm off to bed.

FREDA: Sleep well, dear.

SHELLEY: *(retreating)* Thank you. I'm sure I will. I'm quite worn out.

TAMI: *(calls)* Goodnight. Are you going on this tour, Mr Harrison?

JOE: I guess so. We are booked for it, aren't we honey?

FREDA: We sure are. I wouldn't miss it. I'm told there won't be all that walking. We'll be in the coach most of the time.

TAMI: Do you know who else is going?

FREDA: Some of them. Maisie and llymie Rice and Miss Stoddart. I settled that with them earlier today.
Oh, look over there – those two making for the most secluded corner. See?

TAMI: You mean that couple gazing into each other's eyes?

FREDA: Sweet, aren't they? Honeymooners, I guess. You can't help looking at them, can you? They're called Goor – I saw their name on tomorrow's Coach list. Oh! and these two English ladies, just coming in. *(calls)* Hello! *(whispers)* Do you notice anything odd about them?

TAMI: *(whispers)* They're identical twins!

BETTY: *(approaching)* Hello, Mrs Harrison. Nice to see you again. Good evening, Mr Harrison.

JOE: Good evening. Do I have the pleasure of addressing Miss Lucy or Miss Betty?

BETTY: *(laughs)* Oh, I'm Betty.

LUCY: And I'm Lucy.

TAMI: And I'm none the wiser!

JOE: Oh, let me introduce you. Miss Betty Mannering, Miss Lucy Mannering. Inspector Tami Shimoni.

BETTY:}
LUCY: } How do you do.

LUCY: Inspector? A policeman?

TAMI: I'm afraid so.

BETTY: But how exciting. Are you joining our party, Mr Shimoni?

TAMI:   Well, I'm going on tomorrow's trip anyway. Are you coming?

BETTY:   Yes – oh yes, we are.

LUCY:   We're looking forward to it. Right down into the depths of the Negev desert.

FREDA:   I just hope the heat isn't too unbearable.

BETTY:   That'll be part of the experience, won't it? Come on, Lucy. If we don't start soon, they won't give us any dinner at all. Goodbye.

LUCY:   (retreating) Goodbye. See you tomorrow. Aren't they nice?
They only joined us this afternoon but we got on at once. Shelley! Shelley, my dear. What's happened?

TAMI:   Come and sit down. You look as if you'd seen a ghost. What's the matter?

SHELLEY:   Thank you. I – I don't like this. It's my room. It's been searched.

JOE:   What?

SHELLEY:   It's as though a hurricane has swept through it.

TAMI:   Has anything been taken?

SHELLEY: How can I tell? I haven't looked. I just saw the way it was and came straight down. I should have called the management, I suppose – it was the shock.

TAMI: You can tell them later. Come on.

JOE: Want any help?

TAMI: No. Better leave it to me.

### (FADE OUT. FADE IN)

Ye gods! What a mess. How long will it take you to find out if anything's missing?

SHELLEY: Not long, I suppose. I had very little with me, fortunately. Travelling light. I'd left most of my stuff back in the Ramada at Tel Aviv. I can't imagine what they'd have been looking for.

TAMI: I can.

SHELLEY: You know something about all this.

TAMI: Something. And 1 want to tell you. No, not this moment, but very soon. First I want you to call down to the manager and make the biggest and loudest fuss you can. Then call me, and I'll come down and fetch you.

SHELLEY: You're not staying?

TAMI: No. And you needn't mention me. If they offer to call the police, you agree – but say you'll see them when you're back. Because I'm going to take you out and explain a lot of things.

SHELLEY:   Sounds mysterious. I'm not sure 1 like it.

TAMI:   Nobody does.

SHELLEY:   There's one thing – how in the world could the man have known I wouldn't come back and disturb him?
He didn't make this mess in a hurry.

TAMI:   Easiest of all to answer. Look – come over here by the window. See – a perfect view of the terrace.
They could watch you from here. They could either make sure you were still at the table, or clear out the moment you stood up to leave. Look there are the Harrisons.

SHELLEY:   Well, they were with me all the time. Though I did go straight to dinner from the hairdresser.
They could have... oh, but that's ridiculous.

TAMI:   Possibly. But think about the others who came by while you were down there or just after you'd left us.

SHELLEY:   Hymie and Maisie Rice, for one.

TAMI:   And that honeymoon couple – Goor, is it? Look, still there, holding hands. Oh, and those English ladies, the twins. The Misses Mannering.

SHELLEY:   I'm not sure about that headmistress – Miss Stoddart.
I can't remember if she was there when I arrived or not. But this really is absurd. I can't go round suspecting everyone like this.

TAMI: I'm afraid you may have to, Miss Bernstein. No, I'm damned if I'm going to go on calling you that, I'll call you Shelley, like it or not.

SHELLEY: I like it – Tami.

TAMI: Fine. Make your fuss then. I'll be waiting in my room to hear from you. Then we'll slip out.

**(FADE OUT. FADE IN CAR ENGINE FROM WITHIN CAR INTERIOR)**

SHELLEY: Where are we going?

TAMI: Nowhere particular – just somewhere we can talk.
Thought I'd drive you round to the Liberty Bell Gardens – it's only a little way. We could walk a bit. Oh, and there's an open–air theatre – perhaps something's on.

SHELLEY: First, though, 1 want to know what this is all about.

TAMI: You're entitled. It begins with the man you met on the plane.

SHELLEY: Josh – Joshua? 1 thought so. Do you know him then?

TAMI: No, but I know who he was. I do now, that is – I didn't this morning when 1 came to see you.

SHEILLEY: Was?

TAMI:  He's dead.

SHELLEY:  Oh no! How?

TAMI:  Killed. Stabbed to death – and his body dumped in the middle of Dizengoff on Saturday night. I started investigating it as a normal police enquiry. Then I was told it was all tied in with a top security operation. So I was detached from my usual duties to follow it up.

SHELLEY:  But why was he killed?

TAMI:  Josh was a secret agent. He'd succeeded in penetrating a top security installation in Libya that's producing some sort of biological weapon for use against Israel. We know too little about it, but the little we do know has put the fear of heaven into every boffin and security man in this country. Joshua had managed – God knows how –to obtain either a sample or some message that could give us the answer, enable us to prepare the antidote.
But he was followed on to that plane. We think he sat by you so that he could pass on whatever it was.

SHELLEY:  But he passed on nothing. All that he did do was steal my camera.

TAMI:  We're pretty sure that was a desperate gamble on his part to bring you to our attention. And it came off. But now, of course, the other side also believe you have whatever it is. That's why your room was searched.

### (CAR STOPS. ENGINE OFF)

Look, we're here. Shall we get out and walk?

**(CAR DOORS OPEN AND SHUT.**
**OPEN AIR.**
**OCCASIONAL DISTANT TRAFFIC)**

SI1E.LLEY: What a beautiful evening. It's hard to believe in all that intrigue and violence on a night like this.

TAMI: We get into the gardens through here.

SHELLEY: Why are they called Liberty Bell?

TAMI: Obvious reason – the gardens are a gift from the
USA together with a huge liberty bell as a sort of monument. We'll come to it if we keep walking.
You know, keeping a sort of mini–park like this flourishing in the middle of Jerusalem takes quite an effort. They've had to instal permanent irrigation pipes.

SHELLEY: I've been thinking. What you're really saying is that the other side are desperate to get back whatever it is, and they think I've got it. But I don't, and I haven't a clue where it is. Tami,
I'm scared.

TAMI: No real need. They daren't to anything to you – not while they still think you can lead them to it. But they'll be keeping a close watch – and they're no fools. They'll use people you wouldn't suspect. That's why you must trust no–one – no–one at all.

**(FADE UP SOLO GIRL SINGER AS BACKGROUND,**
**GUITAR BACKING. AT END OF SONG AUDIENCE CLAP)**

SHELLEY: And how do you know ...I mean, how can you be sure of me?

TAMI: I know.

SHELLEY: Thank you.

TAMI: Look – the open–air theatre.

SHELLEY: What a perfect setting. It's like a miniature amphitheatre.

TAMI: Do you want to get closer to the stage? Would you like to sit further down?

SHELLEY: No – let's stay up here on the grass. *(pause)* What's she singing about?

TAMI: *(pause)* Oh – unrequited love.

SHELLEY: Unrequited love? Under the stars in Jerusalem, with the air like wine and the sky like velvet? It doesn't seem fair.

TAMI: Shelley, I must ask you to go back over what happened in that plane. It may be vital.

SHELLEY: I told you everything this morning. Honestly.

TAMI:. I believe you. I'm positive you held nothing back consciously. But think again – was there something you noticed at the time, but didn't think it worth mentioning to me... perhaps because you thought it was irrelevant?

SHELLEY:   Let me think. Well, did I tell you about our little interchange on the subject of my name?

TALI:   You mean about your Hebrew name being Tzivya? Yes, you did.

SRELLEY:   Oh. But there was a sort of sequel to that, you know. It was just as Josh was going back for his hand luggage. I didn't really understand what he meant.

### (CROSSFADE)

JOSH:   You go on. Don't forget – eight o'clock tomorrow. See you – Shelley, or Tzivya, or Rachel, or whoever you are.

SHELLEY:   Goodbye.

### (CROSSFADE)

But why did he throw in Rachel? It puzzled me at the time.

TAM1:   Rachel? No – means nothing to me. I'll think about it. Come on, let's go back to the hotel. It's a full day tomorrow.

### (FADE OUT. FADE IN TELEPHONE RINGING ON DISTORT. RECEIVER LIFTED. PAPPA ON DISTORT)

TAMI:   Pappa?

PAPPA:   Tami?

TAMI:   Yes.

PAPPA:   A minute. I'll carry the phone through to the living room. *(pause)* Well? Any progress?

TAI:. Two things – one tiny, possibly without significance.

PAPPA:  Yes?

TAMI:   The girl remembers Joshua calling her Rachel. Mean anything?

PAPPA:   Nothing. It's not a name we use. I'll bear it in mind – perhaps something will occur. What was the second – about the girl's room being searched?

TAMI:   Yes – but I might have known you'd have heard about that.

PAPPA:   I've got people in 1he hotel. I know there was nothing found – we'd done the job first. A deal more tidily. She also left a suitcase the Ramada hotel in Tel Aviv. Nothing there either.

TAMI:   You really think there's any point in my staying with the girl? You've got her covered without me.

PAPPA:   No – you stay with her. It may seem a waste of time, but
I've a feeling that if we get a break at all, it will be there. Stick close – don't let her out of your sight.

### *(FADE OUT. FULL UP)*

TAMI:   I didn't draw the curtains before falling into bed, and a lance of sunlight woke me early. It was either that, or a thought

– perhaps planted during my talk with Pappa Barzilai – that had been struggling to the surface all night and finally broke through into my conscious mind. It was simple, obvious and devastating. From the point of view of the opposition, Shelley had to die. The reasons were plain, once you thought about it. They didn't need that sample, or the message – whatever it was. All they needed was to prevent it falling into Israeli hands. If Shelley had it, or knew where it was, sooner or later she would tell. So the sooner she was killed, the better. And if by chance she was an uncommitted outsider, then her death was no more than a reasonable precaution. Either way, she was in peril. I had to stick close, just as the old man had said.

## (FADE UP CHEERFUL BREAKFAST CHATTER, CROCKERY)

BETTY:  } *(calls)* Good morning, Mr Shimoni.
LUCY:  } *(calls)* Good morning, Mr Shimoni.

TAMI:  *(calls)* Good morning, Miss …eh …Mannering.

BETTY:  *(laughs – calls)* I'm Betty!

TAMI:  *(calls)* Miss Betty – Miss Lucy. *(pause - low)* Hello Shelley.

SHELLEY:  Oh, hello. What an array! Five different sorts of soft cheeses; one, two, three yoghurts; three different salads, eggs, herring, coleslaw do all Israelis eat this sort of breakfast?

TAMI:  Mostly. The day begins early, and lunch or dinner – whichever they have – is a long way off.

SHELLEY:   Yes, I don't suppose we'll have much during our desert trip today.

TAMI:   I don't know why they do this trip in the summer. It'll be horribly tiring. Shall we sit here?

FREDA:   *(calls)* Good morning, Shelley dear.

SHELLEY:– Morning, Freda. Hello, Joe. *(low)* Someone tried to get into my room last night.

TAMI:   What? Who was it?

SHELLEY:   No idea.

TAMI:   What happened?

SHELLEY:   They tried the door. It must have been the click of The handle that woke me. I'd locked it – thank heaven.

TAMI:   Oh dear. You must be careful, Shelley.

SHELLEY:   Do you care?

TAMI:   I care.

### *(SPOON BANGING ON TABLE. CONVERSATION DIES)*

MAX:   Ladies and gentlemen. Those of you coming on the tour of the Negev should please to hurry. The coach leaves in ten minutes. It is a long day – we must start on time. Oh, one thing. If you have any room, it is not a bad thing to bring something extra to drink.

We'll be carrying supplies on the coach, but the greatest problem of desert travel – especially in the summer – is dehydration.

MAISIE:   *(calls)* My hubby's not usually in much danger of that.

**(LAUGHTER. FADE OUT. FULL UP)**

TAMI:   The coach pulled away from the King David, and I checked up. The ones I'd expected were there – the
Harrisons, the Rices, the twin English ladies, the headmistress, the young Goors, their arms round each other's shoulders, giggling. I sat by Shelley at the back, and watched them all.

**(FADE UP. COACH ENGINE BACKGROUND)**

MAX:   On your left the British consulate serving this part of Jerusalem – situated in the grounds of an ecclesiastical foundation. On your right, the railway station. The railway system was constructed by the British during the period of the Mandate.
Today trains run to Tel Aviv, Netanya, Haifa and points east. Now we turn into the Derech Hebron, the road to Hebron. Past Hebron we go to Beer–Sheva, and then down to the south

**(UP ENGINE. HOLD. CROSSFADE)**

TAMI:   We reached Beer–Sheva about noon, stopped at the four–star hotel for a drink and to stretch our legs, and pushed on. It is only a short distance beyond the town that suddenly the traveller is aware that he is facing out into the unbroken expanse of the desert. Even in our sealed air–conditioned container the change was manifest. Through the broad windows we could see nothing but the undulating brown and sandy billows, one on another, endlessly, with the narrow ribbon of road between them and above a sky of intense blue–white. We could sense the brooding heat which lay on the earth like a heavy blanket, pressing down on the sand and the stones and the rock, as though crushing out all life and movement.

### *(FADE UP – COACH ENGINE BACKGROUND)*

And now we're approaching Sdei Boker – the kibbutz where David Ben Gurion, one of Israel's great Prime Ministers spent his last years.

BETTY: *(calls)* Isn't he buried there, Max?

MAX: That is so, Miss Mannering.

LUCY: *(calls)* Do let's stop and see the memorial, Max.

MAX: Certainly, Miss Mannering. We'll be stopping to have a drink in any case. Anyone else want to walk through the gardens to the Ben Gurion memorial?

FREDA: Is it very far, Max? 1 must preserve my feet.

MAX: No Mrs Harrison. You'll find it no strain at all – and very surprising to find such lush gardens in the middle of the desert. And that view – when you get there it is stunning. You stand high over the desert and see for miles.

MAISIE: Then Mr Rice and 1 will go as well.

HYMIE,: Speak for yourself. I'll have a beer in the café.

JOE: I'll join you.

FREDA:  Men!

MAX:  I'll take the coach to the kibbutz café first, then I'll drive it over to the memorial garden.

LUCY:  Thank you very much, Max.

TAMI:  *(low)* Tell me – those, two old girls. Were they on the plane from Istanbul., by any chance?

SHELLEY:  *(low)* No why?

TAMI:  When did you first see them?

SHELLEY:  Yesterday afternoon. I was in the lobby and I happened to hear them arguing with the receptionist.
I didn't catch it exactly, but it was something about their not having booked, or their booking not being in order. Some mix up. I did wonder then why two old ladies would be travelling about on their own without everything being arranged for them. Why, you don't think...?

TAMI:  I don't know what to think. What I'm afraid of is that someone on this coach isn't all they seem.

### *(FADE OUT. FADE IN COACH ENGINE BACKGROUND)*

MAX:  Nearly at journey's end – the ancient desert city of Avdat, once called Abda. Founded two hundred years before Christ by the Nabateans. The Nabateans were the people who found out how to gather water in the desert. We've got experimental farms trying out their methods. But here, round this corner . . .

**(QUICK FADE OUT. FULL UP)**

TAMI: Suddenly Avdat appeared, climbing a hill on the right – crumbling blocks of geometrically arranged stones which, with time, had taken on the colour and even the texture of the all–encompassing sand.

All the buildings – the fortress, the church, the houses – were roofless, gaping open like the pathetic grin of extreme old age.

**(FADE IN. OPEN AIR)**

MAX: We get out here, at the foot of the hill. Watch how you go.

MAISIE: Well, Hymie, aren't you going to give me a hand?

HYMIE: What do you need a hand for?

MAISIE: My feet hurt.

HYMIE: Feet, hands. Just get off the coach and stop complaining.

MAX: Gather round, everyone. Now these buildings here were the houses of the workers and farmers.

LUCY: I suppose the higher up the hill, the higher up the social scale?

MAX: Precisely, Miss Mannering. Miss Lucy, isn't it?

LUCY. (*delighted*) Quite right, Max. How did you know?

MAX:   I guessed. Follow me, everyone.

FREDA:   Now I must go carefully or I'll surely be sorry.

Tami:   *(low)* Stay back here with me, Shelley. We'll bring up the rear.

SHELLEY:   How do those honeymooners manage to clutch each other's waists and still keep their footing?

TAMI:   Single–mindedness.

MAX:   *(calls)* The houses at:   this level belonged to the wealthier merchants, the officers of the garrison and the priests. As you can see, they are clustered around the public buildings. Look, we are actually walking along the streets of the ancient city.

FREDA:   *(calls)* But these houses – they're so small.

JOE:   *(calls)* What do you expect – split-level ranch homes?

SHELLEY:   *(low)* But it's true. The rooms are tiny.
There's hardly room for a couple of people to turn round.

TAM1:   People were smaller then, probably. Besides they didn't do much more than sleep in there. The life went on in the streets.

MAX:   *(calls)* Now, if you all come up here, you can look over the walls.

LUCY:   *(out of breath)* Oh, Max, it's quite a climb, isn't it? Betty, do come here. What a view.

BETTY: *(out of breath)* I'm getting too old for this kind of thing. Oh, how beautiful – the whole desert spread out before us. Is that our bus down there?

MAISIE: Like a toy, isn't it?

MAX: We can't stay long. I'd like you to see the sunset from up here, but that'll make it too late.

SHELLEY: *(low)* There's something eerie about this place.

TAMI: I know what you mean. It's not only a dead city, it's a city of the dead. All this about us is the result of a final assault in the 10$^{th}$ century when the buildings were destroyed and all the inhabitants killed.

SHELLEY: You're making me shiver.

TAMI: No, that's because the sun is losing its strength. It'll be below those mountains in half an hour.

MAX: Right, back to the coach, everyone.

ALL: *(chatter)*

SHELLEY: *(low)* I must just have a peep into one of the houses, though.

TAMI: I don't think there's time.

SHELLEY: It's all right, they'll wait for us. Over here. The walls of this one are quite high. I suppose this was the living room. What's this?

TAMI:  Looks like a storage jar. Wine or corn. Water, perhaps.

SHELLEY:  Fascinating. To think that this is the thing some woman used – and here it still is... Some woman, two thousand years ago, who lived and loved...

TAMI:  As we live and love.

SHELLEY:  I'm standing in her home. I'm at her kitchen sink.

TAMI:  And sometimes her man would come up behind her *(close)* and catch her round the waist, and kiss the nape of her neck... *(kiss)*

SHELLEY:  *(close)* Tami. *(kiss)*

TAMI:  There's something about this place...

SHELLEY:  You're right – especially now, with the sun beginning to go, down. It gives one a strange feeling. As though we're intruding. Br–rr.

TAMI:  You're cold, darling. You should have brought your coat.

SHELLEY:  It's back in Tel Aviv. I didn't want to drag it around with me. I didn't think it would ever get cold enough to need it. Not in this climate.

TAMI:  Oh but it does at night, even... Say that again!

SHELLEY:  Say what again?

TAMI: What you said!

SHELLEY: That I didn't believe it would get cold enough to need a coat?

TAMI: No. Before that.

SHELLEY: I said I left my coat in Tel Aviv. But you knew that. I... Oh!

TAMI: You left it. But it wasn't in your luggage. You wouldn't have packed a coat.

SHELLEY: No – you're right. I didn't. It's much too big.
I gave it to the porter to store away. I don't know where they put it. Together with the suitcase,
I should think.

TAMI: But when your luggage was searched – it was searched, you know, by both sides – they wouldn't have thought of looking for a separate garment.

SHELLEY: No.

TAMI: Quick! Let's get this straight, while we're alone.
There's not much time. This coat of yours _ has it pockets?

SHELLEY: Yes – two big pockets. And ... and Joshua handled it. He got it down from the rack for me. He could easily have slipped something in one of the pockets.

TAMI: He must have. It's the only...

SHELLEY:   *(screams)* Tami! Watch out! Behind you…

**(THUD. SILENCE. FULL UP)**

TAMI:   I never knew what hit me. I came to very slowly. not understanding where I was, or why I couldn't move. Bit by bit I gathered that my hands were bound tight behind me, and were also attached to whatever was holding my feet together in an unnatural backwards–bent position.

**(FADE IN)**

SHELLEY:   Are you all right? No – don't try to talk yet if you feel bad. 1 thought you were dead, you lay so still.

TAMI:   *(groans)* How long?

SHELLEY:   Not so long, I suppose, though it feels like years. The moon is up – a little new moon. Does that mean it's late?

TAMI:   No – it rises and sets early. What happened? Who did it?

SHELLEY:   It was that couple. The young couple.

TAMI:   The honeymooners? Not as harmless as they seemed.

SHELLEY:   Not at all. The man fetched you a great crack on the side of the head

TAMI:   Don't I know it.

SHELLEY: ... then the girl – she looked so slight and gentle she stood over you with a stone in her hand and said she'd crush your head if I didn't keep quiet while they tied me up. They said they didn't want to kill us. Why was that?

TAMI: Because they know they're expendable – and they'd rather not have murder to answer for, whatever their orders.

SHELLEY: Anyway they trussed us up, then went skipping down the path actually holding hands. I could see them from where I lay. Can you imagine?

TAMI: I suppose they've told Max some tale or other that we'd met friends who were giving us a lift.
Something like that. Mind you, Max should have been on his guard.

SHELLEY: Why – was Max... ?

TAMI: Yes, he knew enough. But 1 can't be sure how sharp he is, or how trustworthy, either. No, we've got to get away – and quickly. I can't see how we can possibly beat that pair back to the Ramada Hotel in Tel Aviv, but we've got to try.

SHELLEY: My hands are just a tiny bit loose. I can move them a little. But that doesn't really help.

TAMI: I don't know, though. Is that your bag over there in the corner?

SHELLEY: Yes – yes, it is.

TAMI: You don't happen to have a pair of scissors in it?

SHELLEY:– Genius. Sheer genius.

**_(FADE OUT. FULL UP)_**

TAMI:   It wasn't easy. It took a long time picking up the bag, opening it, finding the scissors, and then working persistently at the cord that had me trussed up like a chicken ready for the pot. But at last there came the sudden movement that told me the rope had parted. A minute later we were standing, the two of us, in the doorway, looking down at the dead city which lay silvered in the bright– light of the stars and of the tiny sliver of new moon.

**_(FADE IN)_**

SHELLEY:   How are we going to get wherever we're going?

TAMI:   First of all let's get down to the road. Come on.
*(calls)* Watch out.

SHELLEY:   *(calls)* Will we get a lift?

TAMI:   *(calls)* Have to be very lucky. Practically nothing uses this road at night.

SHELLEY:   A camel, a camel – my kingdom, for a camel!
TAMI:   Shelley! You wonderful girl! *(kiss)*

SHELLEY:   You crazy or something? What have I done to deserve that?

TAMI:   That's it! That's exactly it! Perhaps we can get a camel. Come on – hold my hand. We must hurry.

Across the road.

SHELLEY: *(breathless)* What's this? A short cut?

TAMI: *(breathless)* No – it's our best chance. Keep going.

SHELLEY: You sure you know … where you're going?

TAMI: I know where I'm aiming for. Not quite certain it's still there.

SHELLEY: Can't … keep this up … much longer.

TAMI: Nearly there. Keep going.

SHELLEY: Is that a light?

TAMI: Keep going.

### *(DOGS BARKING)*

SHELLEY: *(low – breathless)* Arabs!

TAMI: Bedouin. Ours.

SHELLEY: Ours?

TAMI: Israelis. They've had an encampment round here as long as anyone remembers. You stay here where they can see you, but keep away till I call. They don't like women mixing in men's affairs.

### *(FADE OUT. FULL UP)*

With infinite patience 1 told then as much of the truth as I could – that I was a policeman chasing some dangerous criminals, that I had saved the woman from the robbers, that I had to reach a telephone and could not wait till morning. 1 needed a camel. I offered them all the cash we had. When that was not considered sufficient, I called Shelley over and threw in her watch as a pledge that the camel would be returned or replaced. Finally they were satisfied, and the camel was brought out from behind the encampment, and knelt, grumbling

### (CAMEL. DOGS BACKGROUND)

Let me get up first... there. Now, come on.

SHELLEY:   This animal smells.

TAMI:   Camels do. It's in the nature of the beast. Now watch out as she stands up.

SHELLEY:   (calls) Help! I'm slipping!

TAMI:   (calls) Hold me round the waist. Now, off we go!

SHELLEY:   (calls) It's like being on a horse with ball bearings. I'm being shaken in all directions.

TAMI:   (calls) Save your breath.

SHELLEY:   (calls) I'm going to be sick.

TAMI:   Over the side, then. Look, we're at the road. It'll be easier now.

*(CAMEL'S HOOVES CLICKING IN BROKEN RHYTHM)*

SHELLEY:   We're making terrific speed. Where are we going?

TAMI:   Dimona. I'll be able to phone from there. Damn!

*(CAMEL'S HOOVES STOP)*

SHELLEY:   What is it?

*(CAR APPROACHES)*

TAMI:   Look – over there. There's a car coming this way. We'll get off the road – just in case.

*(CAR ROARS UP AND STOPS, ENGINE RUNNING)*

I don't believe it!

BETTY:   *(calls)* Do come along, you two. What are you waiting for?

LUCY:   *(calls)* We haven't got all night, you know.

TAMI:   Miss Mannering?

LUCY:   Both of us. Now do get off that camel. Betty, Turn the car round.

*(CAR MAKES THREE–POINT TURN. DOOR OPENS)*

TAMI:   You first.

**(DOOR CLOSES. CAR RACING OFF – FROM INSIDE. ENGINE BACKGROUND)**

LUCY:    Don't worry about the speed, incidentally. My sister Betty's an excellent driver. Anyway this is no time for dawdling.

TAMI:   But... how did you...

LUCY:    Quite simple really. Unfortunate that we had to go all the way to Beer–Sheva in the bus, but there was no way to avoid that. Just as well you got this far, though. We'd have had no idea where to look for you in Avdat.

TAMI:   But...

LUCY:    You want explanations. Of course you'll have Gathered that we're... associates... of a certain person. Were, 1 should say, because we're really retired. But he thought this would be just our cup of tea.

TAMI:   I ought to...

LUCY:    No need to phone – we've done it already. He knows what happened. They can't get away with anything now he knows who to watch.

SHELLEY:   You haven't told us what happened – after you left us at Avdat.

BETTY:   Not: difficult, my dear. We simply didn't believe that young pair when they came along with a message from you. You were suppose to have met some friends up in the ruins. Nonsense.

LUCY: We'd had our eye on those two anyway.

BETTY: Yes, much too much of a good thing – all that hand holding and waist clutching. We know quite a bit about–amateur acting – don't we, Lucy?

LUCY: I should say. When we got to Beer–Sheva Betty decided to faint, and I got desperately concerned and insisted we go to the best hotel and stay the night. Max wasn't very keen, but he took us there.
That's where we phoned you–know–who. Incidentally, 1 have a wallet here I'd like you to see. Satisfied?

TAMI: Satisfied.

BETTY: Then once the coach had gone, we went out and stole this car from the hotel car park.

TAMI: You stole...?

BETTY: It was the, first one we found with the ignition key in it. It's really quite fast, isn't it?

### *(UP ENGINE. HOLD. DOWN FOR)*

TAMI: There's a problem. The certain person doesn't know where to look. He won't want to pick up that pair, but he'll have to try to get on the track of the friends they'll send in. He probably won't be able to. We simply must get there first.

BETTY: There? Where?

TAMI: Didn' t I say? The Ramada Hotel in Tel Aviv. Step on it!

*(CROSSFADE TO ENGINE. UP. HOLD. DOWN FOR)*

SHELLEY:   Are those the lights of Tel Aviv – there on the horizon?

TAMI:   Yes. Straight on, through Jaffa. It's quicker.

BETTY:   I know, I know. Less traffic lights. Not that I'm going to stop for any.

*(UP ENGINE. HOLD. SCREECH OF WHEELS NEGOTIATING CORNERS AT SPEED. ENGINE DOWN FOR)*

TAMI:   Try not to kill anyone.

BETTY:   I'll try. It might hold us up.

*(UP ENGINE. CAR HOOTER. CAR SCREECHES TO HALT)*

TAMI:   Out, Shelley! Out! You two wait here. Please!

*(CAR DOOR. RUNNING FEET. HOTEL LOBBY BACKGROUND)*

Police. Where do you store luggage, coats, things like that? Quick, it's urgent.

CLERK:   Down those stairs – service door to the right. But…

TAMI:   Come on.

SHELLEY:   Here. Here it is.

**(DOOR OPENS. CLOSES. SLIGHT ECHO)**

TAMI:   *(low)* Careful. Those racks are for cases. Can you see the coats?

SHELLEY:   There. At the far end. Yes, I think I can see…
Yes, this is my coat.

TAMI:   Let me see Nothing in this pocket. *(pause)*
Bingo! Look at this.

SHELLEY:   A bottle of scent? Show me. "The Serpent's Smile."
It's not mine.

TAMI:   No – and it's not scent, either. This is what we've been looking for – and the others, too. This is what Joshua had to get rid of.

SHELLEY:   *(low – urgent)* Tami! Be careful! Behind you! There's someone with a gun.

PAPPA:   I'll take that, Tami, if you don't mind. Thank you.
Now turn round and come quietly.

TAMI:   Pappa! Pappa Barzilai! What…

PAPPA:   Come over here quietly – both of you. You too, young lady. I haven't got time now for long explanations. And this thing isn't a toy, you know.
I'd hate to use it, but I promise you I would if necessary. Tami, please tell your young lady to obey.

TAMI:   Do as he says, Shelley.

PAPPA:   Now stay there while I just … put this bottle back where it came from. Good. Now we wait. Don't do anything rash, Tami. Try to understand.

TAMI:   Understand!

PAPPA:   *(low)* Yes. Hush! I think they're coming now to collect it. Down, both of you. Don't make a sound.
Trust me... Think!

### *(DOOR OPENS)*

*(whisper)* Think … Remember... You know they have to get it back.

TAMI:   *(whisper)* Then...

SHELLEY:   *(whisper)* My God! The Harrisons!

PAPPA:   *(whisper)* Silence! Not a movement, either of you.

JOE:   *(appoaching)* Don't bother, porter. We can find our stuff ourselves. You know where they put it, honey, don't you?

FREDA:   Sure do. Won't take but a minute. Here it is.

JOE:   Here's your coat too, Freda. You want to take it With you? Might be cold.

FREDA:   All right, Joe. if you think...

JOE:  Nah! Guess you won't need it after all. I've taken that address book you left in the pocket. Come on. *(retreating)* Let's get out of here.

## *(DOOR CLOSES)*

PAPPA:  Mission completed.

SHELLEY:  Well! You – you… And you, Tami! What sort of a man are you? To let him get away with it. And after all that?

PAPPA:  A thinking animal, that's what he is, my dear – if not a quick-thinking one. Still we must make allowances for the knock on the head. How is it, Tami? Bad?

TAMI:– I'll get over it. No, all I'd *been* thinking about was getting here. Of course, you've been at that bottle of so-called scent already.

PAPPA:  Of course.

TAMI:  And replaced the stuff … but what with?

PAPPA:  Replaced? We didn't replace it with anything. We couldn't, or we'd have given the game away. No, the original contents are still there. Except, of course, for a minute drop which I hope they won't miss.

TAMI:  You've lost me again.

PAPPA:  Dear, dear! That must have been quite a whack you got. Can't you see, Miss Bernstein?

SHELLEY:   Not quite. Although there's the start of a glimmer. What was that stuff? Tami didn't tell me.

PAPPA:   No? Well it was – let's say a very unpleasant weapon of war. Rather what the bottle said:   "The Serpent's Smile". Venom, more or less, you might say. If they get their sample back without suspecting that we know about it they'll have no reason to go on experimenting – to find another variation for which we wouldn't have the antidote. Because we'll have one for this, that's certain now – something that'll make the devilish stuff quite harmless.

SHELLEY:   I'm specially glad about one thing.

PAPPA:   What's that?

SHELLEY:   Why, that Joshua didn't give his life in vain.

PAPPA:   No, that is good.

TAMI:   But how on earth …?

PAPPA:   Questions later. I've laid on a table upstairs for a late dinner. We're due there in... fifteen minutes. Save all your questions till then.

**(FADE OUT. FADE IN BACKGROUND CONVERSATION, CROCKERY AND BACKGROUND MUSIC – MODERN HEBREW POP. AT APPROPRIATE POINT IN SCENE, CROSS–FADE MUSIC TO PRE–TIMED VERSION OF EUROVISION SONG "HALLELUJAH". FADE IN)**

TAMI:   What I don't understand is how you managed to get to the coat? The twins couldn't have told you because they didn't know.

Good grief! They must still be outside, unless the police have got them. I told them to wait.

PAPPA:   Sit down, sit down. I've already extricated them from the long arm of the law. The coat? Well, I reached that by two converging routes. Once I'd heard about your little accident up in Avdat, I realised that somehow, Miss Bernstein, you had left slip that you knew where the sample was. Now we were quite sure it wasn't in your luggage in the King David Hotel in Jerusalem, because we'd searched that quite thoroughly...

SHELLEY:   Thank you very much.

PAPPA:   All part of the service. So it had to be in some other article you'd left and that had to be here, in the Ramada Hotel in Tel Aviv. That was path number one. Path number two emerged when I began to think again about every word that Joshua had said to you.
The only inexplicable thing was that mysterious reference to Rachel – remember? It came to me suddenly. Rachel was the first female smuggler as far as I know, the only smuggler mentioned in the Bible. She hid her father's goods in the saddle of her camel.

SHELLEY:   *(bursts out laughing)* Camel? Did you say camel?

TAMI:   *(laughing)* Don't mention camels to us.

PAPPA:   Do you want me to go on?

SHELLEY:   *(fit of giggles)* We haven't told you about our camel ride.

TAMI:   *(laughing)* But do go on.

PAPPA:   To cut a long story short, then, a few minutes after Miss Lucy phoned, the estimable Max came through.

He'd told his passengers some tale about having to report Miss Betty's illness. Incidentally, he thought the English ladies were the villains of the piece – he couldn't make out what was going on. But he'd done the right thing. So I was able to tell him to take his time about coming back. He took the party back by way of the Weizmann Institute in Rehovoth. They got there in the pitch black, and he made a terrible fuss about the mythical floodlighting not being switched on. But it gave me the precious time I needed.

TAMI:  What if that honeymoon pair had also managed to phone, though? Or the Harrisons?

SHELL EY:   That's the saddest part. I liked them.

PAPPA:   The opposition, I'm afraid – specially imported from the States. And they may have phoned for all I know, but I'd taken care of that. You won't know this, but half an hour before you arrived all the traffic in front of the hotel was being held up by the police because some foreign dignitary was leaving. The hotel was blocked off – no–one was being let in or out.

Then a little old gentleman, very distinguished-looking, scuttled down the steps and into a limousine we'd borrowed from the Prime Minister's Office. You know,

Yitzhak from our offfice can look very distinguished, properly kitted out. By then, of course, we'd found your coat, Miss Bernstein, and the sample. But we didn't know what sort of stuff it was. There was a distinct possibility that it was – what do they call those germs, microbes, whatever, that come alive in air?

TAMI:   Aerobic, I think.

PAPPA:   Aerobic, yes. So there was the chance that when we opened that bottle we'd be killing a good many people.

TAMI:  But Joshua must have done something like that operation himself, surely.

PAPPA:  We can't be sure of that but I thought it was possible. So I took the chance. I stationed someone outside the door and said if I wasn't out in five minutes he was to have the placed sealed, the hotel evacuated and to send for a team of back–room boys with respirators. Then I went down the stairs, opened the bottle, and put a couple of drops in a. spare flask. The rest you know.

SHELLEY:  Is anyone ever going to know about all this?

PAPPA:   I devoutly hope not. It's quite enough that we three are able to say "Praise the Lord!"
TAMI:  It's being said for us.

SHELLEY:  What do you mean?

### *(UP MUSIC SLIGHTLY)*

TAMI:   Listen! "Hallelujah", isn't it? From now on I think you and I can call that "our tune".

SHELLEY:  *(laughing)* Indeed we can.

### *(CROSSFADE TO "HALLELUJAH" HOLD. DOWN FOR CLOSING ANNOUNCEMENT. UP "HALLELUJAH" TO END)*

### THE END

# ANNEX

"Jerusalem's Day" – *poem in original Hebrew*

שמואל הופרט

יום-ירושלים

שעות סמוקות בירושלים
בין בוהן-יום לאצבע-ליל,
שמי-ארגמן נושקים שוליך
ובלבך שוכן הצל.

ירושלים, רד הליל, ירושלים.
יבוא עוד יום-ירושלים.
לו אתפלל.

אל שער מט גוהר הערב
בסמטאות העתיקות.
העלטה שוזרה עטרת
מכאב-דורות עמוס-שתיקות.

ירושלים..

הלילה רד על ירושלים
פרשה כנף יונה שחורה.
לילך, עירי, ירושלים,
עורג אל להב-האורה.

ירושלים..

מניין-מתפללים בכותל
המואזין קורא ברום
הצליינים עולים לקבר -
כולם בציפייה ליום.

ירושלים..

## "The Suitcase" – *poem in original Hebrew*

היה זה בחורף ארבעים וארבע.
הגרמנים ציוו: קחו רק את החפצים ההכרחיים ביותר.
עשרים וחמישה קילו לאיש.
אתם נוסעים לעבודה, מזרחה.
לשאר נדאג אנחנו.

עכשיו מוצגת במוזיאון.
יהודית,
שקלטה את חום-כפך, אוטו,
קרה
והברזל חלוד.

הטראנספורט A.L.L.1
נשלח
מטרזינשטאט לרמפה של אושוויץ.

אתה הובלת בקרונות ההם:
שבע פרות, או שלושים חזירים
מאה ועשרים יהודים.

רק המזוודה שלך,
אוטו שווארצקופף,
עלתה לירושלים.

ירושלים, 17.8.1990

254

שמואל הופרט

<u>המזוודה</u>


המזוודה שלך,
אוטו שווארצקופף,
עלתה לירושלים.


מספר הטראנספורט: A.L.L.1
צרוב, בלאק שחור,
בעור
וכן שמך, אוטו,
כתובתך בפראג
ומדבקה של מלון-קיט,
נהרי הטטרה.
פסגות שנתעטפו בשלג
כבטלית,
עצי אשוח דוקרים את השמים הכחולים,
כוי כה,
שבה ושחית?


האב עלית לבדך
אל אחד ההרים,
או נתלוו אליך
אשתך וילדיך?


המזוודה פוערת דפנותיה
וזועקת
ואנשים מביטים בה
ובך,
אוטו.


איפה מטענך?
תחתונים חמים, חולצה, גרבים,
מגבת, מברשת-שניים,
תמונות של אבאמא,
ספר שיריו של היינריך הינה.


255

ISBN 142513754-7

9 781425 137540